DO WORMS HAVE WILLIES?

Sarah Herman and Lucy York

summersdale

DO WORMS HAVE WILLIES?

Written by Sarah Herman and Lucy York

Illustrations by Sophie Goodwin

Summersdale Publishers Ltd
46 West Street
Chichester
West Sussex
PO19 1RP
UK

www.summersdale.com

Printed and bound in Great Britain

ISBN: 978-1-84024-696-4

For our mums and dads, and worms everywhere

Acknowledgements

Herm and Pevs would like to thank...

Carol Baker, for using her eagle-eyed powers to help us and for giggling in all the right places.

The peeps at Summersdale, especially Bertie for making our book look pretty, Anna and Jen.

Bailey and the real League of Titans, for inspiring some of our most bizarre ponderings.

Phillippa York, our wonderful music research assistant.

Each other. It's hard sharing a single brain between two separate bodies, but somehow we made it work.

Contents

Foreword

The most exciting phrase to hear in science... is not 'Eureka!' but rather, 'Hmmm... that's funny...'

Isaac Asimov, American author and biochemist (1920–1992)

A long, long time ago, there were some smart men (there were no smart women; smart women are a relatively recent phenomenon). And those smart men looked at the world and all that was in it and questioned and experimented and scratched their silly little beards, and eventually answered some rather important questions about the way things were.

Of course, living in a time before toasters, the Internet and recycling bins, they weren't the smartest of smart men and a lot of the stuff they said was, well, wrong. Since then many others have stepped up to the plate to serve us with the reliable facts that we hunger for, and time and time again we have been let down.

Whether they're harping on about the shape of the earth, life on Mars or the number of jelly beans you can fit in a phone box, they're usually getting it wrong. Lately, we've stopped listening. Sometimes the questions you really want answering are so far down the smart guys' list of priorities that you just have to answer them yourself, or read this book and have them answered for you.

We may not wear science goggles (sometimes we do), carry out groundbreaking research or have PhDs, but what we lack in actual knowledge, qualifications and height we make up for with enthusiasm, flair and sheer stupidity... so we're not that different from those original smart guys, then. Except the beards – we don't have beards.

This is a book of sentences filled with nonsense composed by two very sensible typists. We hope you enjoy it very much.

Sarah Herman and Lucy York

SKIN, BONES AND BODILY FLUIDS

Could paper cuts kill you?

If you knew the potential danger of paper cuts, you wouldn't be reading this book. In fact, you'd never have picked it up in the first place, because you wouldn't dare to set foot in a book shop. Most bookworms remain blissfully unaware of the danger they put themselves in every time they settle down for a good read, as death by paper cut is an extremely rare and little-reported occurrence.

The sensation of a paper cut is familiar to most – the initial shock and pain, the feeling of outrage, the niggling after-sting, aggravated by contact with liquid, and the final shedding of the affected strip of skin, which is unimpressively small in proportion to the amount of discomfort it has caused and how much you've whinged about it. But for those unlucky enough to have been infected with the Papyrus virus, the suffering doesn't end there.

This vile disease enters the bloodstream through the fingers and quickly infiltrates the entire epidermis. The viral cells latch onto skin cells and absorb their moisture, leaving the outer layer of skin dry and crinkly. Any movement the sufferer makes dislodges a shower of skin-flakes akin to chronic dandruff and is accompanied by an excruciating rustling noise which makes simple actions, such as sneaking into a cinema after the film has started, impossible. Once infected, there's no hope for the patient, and they will continue to deteriorate until there's nothing left of them but a shrivelled-up crisp that floats away on the slightest breeze.

Scientists have traced this disease as far back as the time of the pharaohs in ancient Egypt and it has been recorded in paper-making societies ever since. The virus is estimated to be present in only one in every five million sheets of paper but, frankly, we're not taking any chances — we never pick up a book or go into the stationery cupboard without donning our marigolds first.

What is a monobrow for?

The monobrow – a single, strong arch of hair reclining above the ocular cavities – once stretched across the faces of kings, military leaders and fashion-conscious blokes the world over. Now, it is nothing more than a third-rate culinary ingredient found in Scotland's worst dining rooms. Oh, how it has fallen.

Long ago, when men were men and swords were brandished to settle pub brawls, the monobrow was an essential element of facial hair favoured above (literally) the beard or fancy 'tache. Rather than wax-strip away their furry friend, men would hope that theirs would be the thickest and most prominent in the land. The reason being that the brow provided a necessary net to catch excessive sweat, flying debris and stray food accrued during your typical tavern punch-up. The brow muscle, combined with a large 'mono', was known to be capable of supporting the weight of an entire slice of ham (the equivalent of a modern-day packet of pork scratchings).

As times changed, and bouncers became commonplace, the brow faded into obscurity amongst stylish, well-bred men. Some simply familiarised themselves with the latest hair removal creams and washed their central clump down the drain, while others, who needed the money, sold their shorn hair to world-class chefs who claimed the androgenic fibres (when added to salmon mousse) worked wonders for the sophisticated palate. Post-war ration-conscious cuisine, however, soon put an end to this delicacy, and now it is only used as a sauce-thickening ingredient in a few suspect Glaswegian restaurants.

The monobrow did see a brief revival in the 1970s when American children fashioned 'brow bridges' out of beaver fur and sticky tape to create the illusion of a single hair slug. Their *Blue Peter*-esque efforts were in reverence of Monoman — known in Japan as Mr Mono — a popular comic-book hero.

Can you Knit a Jumper out of belly button fluff?

In this age of environmental awareness, when everyone marches to the tune of 'Reduce, Reuse, Recycle', the question shouldn't be whether you can knit a jumper out of belly button fluff but why more people aren't doing it already. And in a sweatshop in the outer reaches of Mongolia, that's precisely what one enterprising, formerly nomadic tribe have been up to.

Belly button fluff is formed when fibres from clothing get caught in the hairs of the navel and collect to form a ball of 'fluff'. Male members of the Mongolian Bindhi tribe are genetically prone to large belly buttons, and as they predominantly wear clothing made of thickly woven yak hair for insulation against the harsh climate, their fluff yield is exceptionally high. The women of the tribe originally began collecting the fluff from their husbands and using it to plug cracks in the walls to keep out draughts, but on a long and boring winter's night, one woman discovered that the fluff could be teased out into a thread of surprising strength and spliced with other threads to form a length of yarn.

With an endless supply of wool and a stack of *Woman's Own* magazines that had been sent to them by a well-meaning Women's

Institute group in Barnsley, there was no stopping them as they knit-one-purl-oned through a wealth of knitwear patterns from the 1970s. The chief quickly realised the earning potential of this new craze amongst the womenfolk, and the tribe settled down and began focusing their energies on the manufacture and export of the garments.

The Navel Knits have been selling well in Fairtrade outlets around the world, and there are plans to extend the range to tea cosies and toilet roll holders. A Scandinavian investor is funding research into ways to dye the wool different colours, but at the time of writing the sole output colour is the natural blue of the untreated fluff.

How can I make myself immune to tickling?

Those among us who are ticklish will know that nothing compares to the squirming feeling you get inside when a would-be tickler approaches with arms outstretched and fingers a-wriggling. It's a fine line between pleasure and pain, and the tickle that makes you giggle can quickly become the tickle that makes you lash out violently at the tickler, or even wet yourself. The trouble is that most ticklers just don't know when to stop. And who can blame them? One can only imagine the power and sense of self-importance they feel when they're getting more laughs out of you than a top stand-up comedian could manage on a world tour.

The good news is that salvation is at hand, thanks to one man who decided that enough was enough and made it his life's mission to find a way of neutralising the ticklish gene. Astel Wrigglebottom was a pale and feeble child, the youngest of a family of four brothers who would seize every available opportunity to wrestle him to the ground and give him a good tickling. The treatment continued at school, where he was subjected to many a tickle-fest, his uncontrollable girlish laughter giving the school bullies much amusement.

Growing up on a farm and spending a lot of time hiding from his tormentors in the chicken coop, he often wondered why his fowl friends weren't tickled by their own feathers. On a trip to France as a teenager, after eating a large number of omelettes, he noticed that his reactions to tickling were greatly reduced. He set about identifying the element in eggs that would make him, and other sufferers, immune to tickling.

The fruit of his labour, Dr Wrigglebottom's Anti-tickle Pickle, is available to buy on the Internet today. It contains free-range eggs that are pickled over a very long period of time in a special formula, causing the anti-tickle agent contained in eggs to intensify. Once ingested, the agent passes into the bloodstream and moves to the nerve endings, disabling the tickle receptors. Tests have shown that by eating one pickle with each meal, every day, you will be able to withstand up to 27 minutes of tickling without cracking so much as a smile. But if you're eating that many pickled eggs a day, your farts are going to smell so rank that no one's going to want to get within tickling range of you anyway, as poor Astel Wrigglebottom soon found out.

If trapped there indefinitely, could a baby scratch its way out of the womb?

NB: *This answer contains descriptions that some readers may find disturbing, especially pregnant ones.*

There's a good reason babies grow fingernails inside the womb.

In the large majority of pregnancies everything goes swimmingly. The baby grows, the baby is born and the baby is healthy. In a small minority of cases (don't worry, it really is only a few expectant mothers a year), unknowingly to her, the mother's body refuses to push the baby down the birth canal. She experiences no contractions or pain and therefore does not realise the baby is ready to be born and carries on as normal. The baby meanwhile is ready to get out and soon, realising it's not going down the tube it was meant to, and that no one is coming to get it, it begins using the womb as a bench press; flexing its muscles and practising some serious punching that Bruce Lee would be proud of. To the mother, this just feels like a bout of hard-core baby kicking, and she thinks nothing of it.

After a few days of intense workouts, the baby is ready to break free from the restricting uterus and see some daylight. It waits until the mother is sleeping, as this is when her heart rate is slowest and her muscles are most relaxed, making them softer and more easily destructible. Manoeuvring itself into place and warming up its muscles, the baby goes for a straight one-inch punch, powering up through the layers of flesh and organs in its path. If the baby has aligned itself correctly, none of the major organs will be touched by the arm and a small hole (approximately five centimetres in diameter) will appear in the mother's belly. Usually at this point the mother will wake up from the pain, but as she scrambles around her bedroom desperately trying to pack her overnight bag for her hospital stay, the baby's fingernails come in handy, as it scratches its way out of the small space, stretching and tearing the skin as it goes.

In some cases the father-to-be has fought to push the baby's arms back through the hole, preventing it from leaping out *Alien*-style. It is more common, however, for the mother to pass out from the shock, especially in the absence of the father or anyone else, and then the baby is free to wriggle out of the space, snap the umbilical cord with its superior arm strength and drag itself to safety.

Self-birthing is currently within the bounds of the law and police officers are required not to treat the incident as a crime on arrival. One mothers' action group is trying to bring about a law that allows victims of this type of birth to sue their own children for the physical scars and emotional trauma they cause.

If I pick my nose too much, will my head cave in?

Ah, the surreptitious pleasures of nose-picking – the suspense of probing your nostril, the excitement felt at locating pickers' gold, and the satisfaction at extracting a prize bogey and flicking it at some unsuspecting passer-by... but would you still do it if you knew the effect it was having on your brain?

Though we hate to be the bearers of bad news, we can reveal that the Dried Mucus Theory is nothing but an urban myth propagated by ardent and somewhat desperate nose-pickers in the sixteenth century. The little green nuggets you've been merrily plucking from your nose since your playground years are in fact fragments of your brain.

Every so often, clusters of dead brain cells break away and gradually slide down into the nasal cavity, where they will remain lodged until a flow of mucus flushes them out, unless, of course, you pick them out first. The scraping action of a finger moving around inside a nostril stimulates the discharge of further brain cells. If done too often and the supply of dead cells is exhausted, the brain will go into overdrive and begin to release living cells. Once initiated, this process is hard to stop and whole sections of the brain may be lost at once.

Thankfully, the social stigma attached to nose-picking has ensured that things very rarely get to this stage, but there was one reported case of a picker from Norway who suffered irreparable brain damage. Little Heather Snotmundsen continued to pick at her nose, despite warnings from her parents, until the whole right side of her brain was eaten away. When she began to produce particularly hard and crunchy specimens her parents realised that her skull had begun to disintegrate too, and she was rushed to hospital. Unfortunately, it was too late to stop one side of her head from collapsing. Aside from suffering the loss of some of her vital cognitive abilities, Heather can no longer go outside without her head covered, and has been subjected to the shame of wearing garish beanies knitted by her well-meaning aunts ever since.

Why do sperm look like tadpoles?

Believe it or not, human sperm never used to resemble the common pond tadpole. The fruit of a man's loins was once the shape of a miniature hunting arrow; a small, sharp arrowhead, with a sleek, straight tail end with feathery fibres to guide it on its journey towards the egg. Sperm of yesteryear were strong and skilled swimmers, and as a result fertility problems were rare and multiple births commonplace. As easy as it would be to assume that the change in shape over time is due to a few too many real-life 'Princess and the Frog' incidences, this is not the case. The truth, however, is slightly more disturbing.

Although scientists haven't pinpointed exactly when the sperm transformation occurred, some time in the third century BC a change in the global climate caused an extended rainy season across the southern hemisphere. Land that was normally productive became waterlogged and unusable; many farmers' livelihoods were snatched away by the bad weather. In a drive to combat this, tribe leaders asked their people to come up with more inventive ways to use the wetland, and while many farmers turned to rice production, a large percentage found the jelly-like eggs of the marshland frog the ideal way to create wealth out of the water.

Frogspawn was a must-have comestible – the protein-rich jelly and sugary undeveloped tadpoles went perfectly with rice and thus was spread on rice cakes, and, when cooled to a sufficiently low temperature, made the perfect summer's day treat. But the frogspawn-munchers weren't to know that when they chowed down on the live tadpoles, the little wrigglers were set free into their bodies and found their way into men's testes. Their size meant they were able to bully the tiny human sperm into looking just like them, and soon the arrowheads disappeared, as did the feathered tails, until all that was left was a bunch of teeny, tiny tadpole sperm with reduced mobility, and a bad pondweed smell.

Is there anything I can do to safeguard myself against spontaneous combustion?

The causes of spontaneous human combustion (SHC) are much disputed in the scientific community, but the many theories surrounding this phenomenon point to one solid fact: you can avoid spontaneously combusting by maintaining a physically and emotionally healthy lifestyle. Stick to these guidelines to ensure you're not the main attraction at this year's bonfire night.

1) Avoid the consumption of alcohol and wheat and dairy products.

When a high level of bacterial fermentation occurs in a confined space (such as your stomach) and the resulting heat has no means of escape, temperatures can rise above ignition point. If sufficient oxygen is present, combustion can occur. Steer clear specifically of cheap ciders, smelly cheeses and organic chocolate cheesecake flavoured milkshakes.

2) Eat healthily and exercise.

Another suggested explanation for SHC is the 'wick effect', in which clothing absorbs melted human fat and then burns at a steady rate. Don't want to end up as a human candle? Then say no to seconds of sticky toffee pudding and get on that treadmill!

3) Exfoliate, cleanse and moisturise.

In certain conditions, such as walking over a nylon carpet on a cold, dry day, wearing horsehair slippers, the average human can build up an electrostatic charge of up to 20,000 volts. This would normally be discharged through the tips of your hair – but not if you have excessively dry skin, in which case you could conduct up to 30,000 volts. Once this kind of static ignites your clothing, you've only got seconds before you're reduced to an ugly stain on the office carpet. Keep static flashes at bay by investing in a good exfoliating scrub and moisturising cream, and embarking on a daily skincare routine.

4) Wear clothing made of non-synthetic materials such as cotton.

The impact of both the wick effect and static flashes can be significantly reduced by wearing clothing which is not highly flammable.

5) Be yourself, be happy.

Perhaps the most tenuous theory of all is that being severely emotionally distressed can trigger a biological process in which the hydrogen and oxygen contained within a person's cells are ignited in a series of mitochondrial explosions. Stay on an even keel by avoiding stressful situations, and seek counselling (or visit a theme park) immediately should you begin to feel depressed.

If you do all this then you should be in the clear. However, if you at any time detect an overwhelming rise in your body temperature and suspect that you are about to spontaneously ignite, you can halt the process by taking one of two emergency actions: submerge yourself in water by flinging yourself fully clothed into a bath or other body of water; or roly-poly your way down a large hill – the smothering effect will inhibit the flames, and you'll have a lot of fun.

Can you get seasick on a waterbed?

In the days when flower power and UV posters were all the rage and having an Afro was not considered ironic, a waterbed was the ultimate bedroom accessory. Giant wobbling mattresses graced the rooms of the rich and famous and those lucky enough to snap one up from their local furniture emporium for a hefty sum. Despite claiming to help people with back pain, migraines and even weight issues (the constant movement of the body during sleeping hours was thought to equate to a two-hour workout), and coming down considerably in price after the introduction of imported Chinese waterproof fabrics, it's impossible to pick yourself up a waterbed from DFS these days. The reason? They're currently illegal in 31 countries and it is thought only four manufacturers remain in business – all located in South America.

Seasickness was a common problem for waterbed owners, who would regularly wake in the night feeling nauseous, dizzy and breathless. Scientists and doctors, who OK'd the waterbed and gave it their stamp of product-safety approval, were quick to criticise the individual sleepers who came forward to lodge complaints, blaming their drug-taking, fabric softeners and sexual appetites for the sickness. But as more and more people began demanding their money back from the beds' producers – in an international scandal known today as 'Waterbed Gate' – they were forced to re-test the beds to back up their claims. What they discovered shocked the furniture industry to the core…

After carrying out a series of case studies with waterbed users the research team learnt that people who spent more than seven hours in bed a night were not only experiencing the seasickness side effects commonly reported but were also starting to develop unusual breathing patterns, flaky skin and webbing of the toes. Their prolonged exposure to the beds – which effectively recreate the sensation of being on water, combined with the tactile sensation and sounds of water in motion – were tricking the sleepers' minds into believing they were creatures of the sea. One lady who was bedridden and only left her waterbed for thirty minutes a day was photographed for an American tabloid magazine with her new set of gills on display. Needless to say, governments around the world were quick to add waterbeds to their list of illegal pieces of furniture.

How many facelifts could a person survive?

Don't panic, facelift lovers – you've probably got a few more left in you yet… But if you are a surgery addict, you might want to read this before you book yourself in for your next op.

Essentially, a facelift involves peeling back the layers of skin from the blood vessels and tissue of the face and stretching them further than their original position. Due to the skin's elastic nature, there is considerable room for manoeuvre, especially with older, wrinkled skin. A smooth, taut-looking face is the optimum result. The small scars are usually hidden by the hairline, or behind the ears, so your nip 'n' tuck won't be on display for all to see – that is, of course, unless you take things a few steps too far.

In Hollywood (where else?), Lilly Lollipop, an ageing glamour model, treated herself to a facelift every two years throughout her fifties and sixties. She found that unless she booked herself in immediately after an op, the waiting list for her particular surgeon meant it could be nearly three years before she could get another appointment with him. But the use of heavy make-up, exposure to harsh UV rays and the stress of constantly worrying about her looks meant that the youth-enhancing effects of each facelift barely lasted two years anyway.

Despite Lilly's surgeon expressing his concerns during her tenth surgery appointment – he noticed that skin cells around the cheekbones and chin were not regenerating, creating areas of extreme fragility – she insisted he go ahead with the procedure. But when she came back for number eleven, he turned her away, refusing to ignore his Duty of Care as an MD. Lilly jetted off to South America, after finding a rogue surgeon willing to take on her face. Sadly, she never made it to the operating table. During the flight, a combination of the weight of Lilly's fake tanning lotion and the high pressure in the cabin caused Lilly's facial bones to break through the thinner areas of skin, literally tearing her face apart. She died of a heart attack, which doctors later attributed to a sudden rise in her anxiety levels after she caught a glimpse of her own reflection in the plane's window.

Do we need a Middle finger?

If you were to lose your middle finger in a freak meat-cutting or door-slamming incident, you would undoubtedly experience some discomfort and awkwardness, but nothing that would prevent you getting on with the most essential everyday tasks (though it would put you at a serious disadvantage in a match of paper, scissors, stone). But for our cave-dwelling, food-foraging ancestors it was a very important part of the anatomy indeed.

Our central and longest digit is but a shadow of the impressive size it once was, averaging at five times the length of the index finger in adult male Neanderthals. Its purpose was two-fold: firstly, it was used to poke into holes in fallen tree trunks and winkle out the juicy white grubs which provided an important source of protein in our ancestors' diet. Secondly, it was used to ruthlessly flick birds from their nests in order to steal their eggs, in a motion known to anthropologists as 'flipping the bird'.

It was also a symbol of virility and dominance, with the size of the digit denoting hierarchy within tribes, and a raised middle finger was seen as a direct threat or challenge to other males.

Increasingly efficient hunting weapons and techniques meant that the middle finger fell out of use and over time evolved into the smaller version we are familiar with today, but the gesture remains just as offensive as it was to our hairy forefathers.

An online social networking group recently tried to promote the middle finger in the hope of having it rebranded as 'the most important finger' by the Association of Digit Dexterity – currently the number one spot is held by the pinky! They suggested a number of tasks that the middle finger was essential for. As well as the ultimate swearing gesture, the lengthy list included: tenpin bowling, archery, a successful wave and the gym-junkie's favourite – middle-finger press-ups.

Do bad dancers really make bad lovers?

Contrary to popular belief, men who can't shake it on the dance floor are often surprisingly good at pleasuring their partners in the bedroom*. In a recent reader survey, a popular women's magazine asked its subscribers to name the qualities that made someone good in the sack. The three most popular answers were: 'generosity', 'stamina', and 'open to new ideas'. While dancers may have good rhythm and score points for flexibility (which is always a bonus!) men who hover on the periphery of the dancing area clutching their drinks, or who look more David Brent than Patrick Swayze when they do actually hit the tiles, usually have these qualities by the bucket-load.

Generosity is an easy one to see. These are the guys who will happily hang back while their lady shakes her ass into another guy's crotch. They'd rather you bumped and grinded with everyone else in the place and had a good time than embarrass you with their moves. Either that or they're such a generous, accommodating person that they brave the dance floor in spite of their failings, just to make you smile.

As for stamina, well, they'd need it just to hang out by the bar the whole night while you go off and have a good time. When your feet are aching at the end of the evening, they'll be the one carrying you home, rather than complaining about their own aching tootsies. And they don't need an evening's worth of Beyoncé and Justin tunes to keep them up all night...

And finally, are bad dancers adventurous? Well... unlike their Fred Astairian mates, who are all 'shuffle, ball change' and forever having to steal the limelight with their newest moves, your two-left-footed machine will be untamed, unstructured and unbelievable between the sheets. He won't need to know the routine beforehand or be shown an instructional DVD starring the latest soap-opera reject.

So the next time you giggle with your mates about the guy trying to body-pop who looks more like a spaniel with a tic, don't be so quick to judge – he just might be worth taking for a walk.

*No matter whether a woman can shimmy like she's in the cast of *Chicago* or spends more time standing on other people's feet than her own, she'll definitely be a great lover... women always are.

If someone's heart stopped could a lightning strike revive them?

Though the chances of it happening are pretty slim, if a person was struck by lightning during the three-minute window following the moment their heart stopped, the shock could restart their heart. Provided that person's nervous system wasn't completely fried by the massive voltage that passed through them, they would be able to get up and walk away and continue to live a normal life.

Or should we say an *almost* normal life. Though they wouldn't realise it at first, the lightning strike would have caused certain irrevocable changes to take place. The most noticeable difference to onlookers would be their hair, of course, which would be so enormously big as to put any backcombing fan of The Cure to shame. Secondly, they would develop an allergy to electricity – just being in the vicinity of an electrical appliance would give them a migraine and bring them out in an unpleasant rash. Perhaps most bizarrely, they would also lose all inhibitions (cue much naked parading and outdoor sex) and the power of speech.

DO WORMS HAVE WILLIES?

Very few lightning revivals have taken place, and you are unlikely ever to have the chance to meet with someone who's experienced one. Because of their allergy to electricity, these survivors have all been relocated to an abandoned research station in the Arctic Circle, powered by six obedient polar bears on a running machine. Their small community has very little contact with the outside world, but a recent journalist sent there to make a documentary reported some very strange activities, including community members wandering around undressed (except on Saturdays when outrageous fancy-dress costumes were obligatory) and the construction of what appeared to be some sort of saucer-shaped flying craft. The documentary was never finished because the subjects were uncooperative – they appeared to be completely absorbed in using an old Morse code transmitter they'd found to send messages into space.

Why do people coo over babies?

In Bangkok Palace, in the heart of Thailand's capital, tourists queue for hours to catch a glimpse of the tiny Emerald Buddha, a small statue that sits atop an extravagant golden tower. Found on the west coast of Koh Lanta by monks in the 1920s, it was believed to be a sacred ancient relic, sent to the people by Buddha as a sign of future prosperity. The answer to your question lies in this green Buddha baby.

Pirates roaming the South China seas in the eighteenth century were always on the lookout for buried treasure. They would stop off at islands for food and supplies, ravish a few local ladies and make their merry way back onto the high seas. Pirate romances were not unheard of: when Captain Dock Green fell in love with a Haitian girl, she joined him and his crew as they travelled the globe. She soon fell pregnant and gave birth to a son, but was brutally murdered by a rival pirate gang shortly afterwards. Green was distraught, but decided to raise the child alone.

One stormy night, Green's ship ran aground. Green, his son and a few crew members survived, washed up on an uninhabited island. But with no food to eat they soon became agitated by the baby's cries and began to debate over whether to eat the child. It was then that a parrot landed on Green's shoulder and cawed loudly, squawking at the baby in a high-pitched call unlike anything the pirates had heard before. The baby soon quietened down and began gesticulating wildly towards a nearby cave. The crew followed the baby's signals and soon enough uncovered a cavern of jewels, gold and food supplies.

Not long after, they were rescued by passing fishermen and returned to their home countries the richest men alive, where they told tales of the parrot's call, the baby and the riches it had found them. Although Green's child never lived beyond infancy his legacy remains in the weird noises people still make at babies... and the Emerald Buddha statue in Bangkok's palace – a figure made by pirates in tribute to the Green baby who found treasure.

Has anyone ever cried a river?

Most people are familiar with the tale of the Ethiopian Puddle Boy – the child who cried enough tears to form three small puddles, providing water to feed a dying orange tree whose nutrient-rich fruit helped an entire village survive a deadly famine. But despite the enormity of his feat, his tear-jerking efforts pale in comparison to those of the considerably less famous Elah Nilus, an Egyptian servant who ritually washed the feet of pharaohs with his ocular fluids in a sacred cleansing ceremony.

Each day he would rise at dawn to fill an urn with his tears before breakfast in time for the pharaoh's morning foot scrub. Inexplicably, he was able to produce large amounts of tears through concentrated meditation. Occasionally, if his fellow servants told a particularly funny joke or he'd had a great night out, he would need to stub his own toes or watch a local criminal being stoned to death to encourage the liquid release.

After sixty years of devout service, moisturising the pinkies of four royal leaders, Elah was ready to retire. On the day of his last foot bath a trio of kitchen porters couldn't stop cracking chuckle-worthy one-liners and, excited about his upcoming leaving bash, Elah was struggling to squeeze out tears. After reminding himself of the pittance of a pension he would soon be receiving and the fact he'd recently become impotent, the tears finally began to flow, only this time they refused to stop. Hard as Elah tried his incontinent tear ducts continued to flow until his clothes were dripping and puddles had begun to form around his feet. And still the tears came. Soon Elah was being carried in a river of his own tears out of the palace doors and off into the desert, never to be heard of again.

The river remained, but, embarrassed by the expense caused to the taxpayers in order to fund the palace refurb, the pharaoh declared he himself had prayed to the gods for the river to ease the spot of drought they were having and, clearly, his prayers had been answered. Although no one ever spoke of the Egyptian crier again (under the pharaoh's orders), in honour of Elah Nilus he named the river 'The Nile'.

Do wisdom teeth really contain wisdom?

Appearing as they do in humans between the ages of 16 and 24, when most young people are studying for school or university exams, it would be pretty handy if the late-arriving third molars did bring wisdom, or at least the odd trigonometry formula. Unfortunately, there are no epiphanies in store for you if you stare ritualistically at your own wisdom teeth in a well-positioned mirror. The late-appearing buggers will cause you nothing but aches, pains and, if you're lucky, the odd day off school/work.

In developed countries, preventive removal of these molars is increasingly common, even in cases where there is no evidence of overcrowding in the patient's mouth. But a recent study showed that there is little or no scientific evidence to support this practice, and that sixty per cent of wisdom teeth extractions could be avoided.

So why *are* dentists plucking out wisdom teeth left, right and centre? The fees they earn from such extractions are neither here nor there – it's what they do with the teeth once they've pulled them out that's funding their pensions. Although it's hard to imagine anyone with any sense paying over the odds to get their hands on your funny-looking back teeth, these molars are selling like hot cakes on the black market to modern-day witch doctors.

The teeth are used in a ritual similar to bone-reading, during which the teeth are discarded onto a mat and the patterns they form are 'read' in order to provide answers to questions which can range from 'What lottery numbers will come up this week?' to 'Is my husband cheating on me?' or even completely spurious ponderings such as 'Do worms have willies?' Yes readers, we are indeed in possession of a set. Sadly, our publishing contract means that we can't share the secret tooth-reading technique with you. As for whether the teeth really contain wisdom – we'll leave that for you to decide.

THE STUFF OF NATURE PROGRAMMES

Do worms have willies?

The willy is a marvellous biological form. From the mighty elephant's tree-trunkian cannon to the anteater's three-headed wonder-shaft, there's not a testosterone-fuelled animal out there that can't look down between its legs and swing around whatever it sees with some level of pride. That is, of course, except the humble worm.

The general populace believe that the worm is an asexual creature, or that, like its snake cousins, its procreation tackle is hidden up some sneaky hole to prevent friction burns when Mr Worm is on the move, popping out just for special occasions. The general populace… is wrong.

There is a good reason why worms are blind, and that they bear such a striking resemblance to a pink, wriggly male member. For that is exactly what they are. Yes, ladies and gentlemen, worms *are* willies. The skinny, smooth, slime-secreting wrigglers that we see in our gardens are all male worms. The females are buried deep below ground and are brown, round and spongy in texture. Just like in any fantastical patriarchal society, the blokes go out to work, squirming around in mud and filth to find food and nesting debris for their mates. One female is shared by approximately twenty males to increase the chance of reproduction. This ratio is reflected in their offspring, where the male chromosomes are dominant. The men risk life and their only organ in order to keep the egg-bearers safe from birds and garden trowels and return home to feed and fertilise the females.

Because of their simple mud-tunnelling lifestyles, the male worm really has no need for eyes, arms or any other appendages. And it's just as well that he can't see where he's going when it's time to perform his manly duties and insert his head inside the female in order to deliver his load. Although it is very rare to see the mating process because of the females' camouflaged colouring and the speed at which copulation takes place, scientists believe it is the front end, and not the tail, that takes one for the team, because the tail is needed to fight off the queue of nineteen other impatient suitors.

It is said that if inebriated, scorpions will go mad and sting themselves to death. Are there any other creatures that can't handle their drink?

The venom of a scorpion, whilst toxic to other living organisms, is not harmful to the scorpion itself or others of its own kind. This is lucky for the scorpion, for although they aren't known drinkers, ingestion of alcohol can cause them to behave in a severely erratic fashion: one scorpion who'd had one drop too many is reported to have met a tragic end after picking a fight with a spitting cobra.

Immoral, irrational and uninhibited actions have also been observed in other members of the insect kingdom when under the influence of alcohol, not least of all the common fruit fly. When students at the Pennsylvania State University decided to see what would happen if they got a group of male fruit flies high on ethanol fumes by placing them in a specially created chamber named the 'Flypub', they were both surprised and a little embarrassed by the results. As soon as the fumes had taken effect, the flies exhibited signs of arousal and began to engage in homosexual courtship activities. Over the course of the experiment, repeated exposure increased their sensitivity to the drug, and by the end of the week the students were witnessing full-on male-on-male fly orgies.

Inspired by this groundbreaking research, another group of students at Glasgow University tried a similar experiment on woodlice by placing them in a shallow trough filled with XXX Special Brew, christened the 'Bug Boozer'. On the first day the group recorded 'ill-advised attempts at dancing' and by the second, 'repeated and frequent expulsion of waste matter'. On the third day the tests were called to a halt when it was decided that the woodlice had become 'tired and emotional'.

Why would you flog a dead horse?

Most people think that when a horse is dead it is, in fact, dead. In most cases this is true. In some cases – and these have been widely reported by a number of questionable journalists – the horse is only 'nearly dead' or 'super mortis'. As with a few other large mammals including giraffes and rhinos, when the central heart stops beating and shuts down a number of reserve hearts kick into action.

Located at various pump points around the body (the number and positioning depend on the animal's size and shape) these secondary pumps can keep a horse moving for up to three hours after it is actually dead. The heart switch-over is noticeable to any onlooker, marked by a brief faint-like collapse and a period of convulsions. It is during this time that some cultures that rely heavily on the horse as a working animal, or those who revere it as a god, will choose to gently flog or pat the dead animal with ceremonial branches to encourage blood flow to the pump points, returning it to life for a few final hours of celebration and worship, or to get a last three hours' worth of work out of it.

For the Brinto people of South Botswana the 'pump period' allows the owners to shower their special breed of African shire with gifts, food and praise; thanking it for all its work and wishing it well in the afterlife. People who have recently lost loved ones are encouraged to write messages to the spirits of their parted family members in chalk on the horse's body – this is thought to bring comfort and peace to the dead as well as providing the shire with a pleasant tickling sensation as it prepares to leave this world for the next.

Are lobsters good singers?

In modern times, lobsters have earned their reputation as vocalists largely for inglorious reasons. Ask any gourmet chef and he will tell you that the best way to cook a lobster is by boiling it alive, a technique which is practised in restaurants across the globe. Sadly, this means that the only performance most people will ever hear a lobster give is the heart-wrenching 'Lament of the Boiling Lobster'. But a couple of thousand years ago, in ancient Peru, you would have heard lobsters singing a quite different tune.

The Moche people, who populated northern Peru from around AD 100 to 800, worshipped the sea and all its creatures. Lobsters in particular were central to their belief system, and featured prominently in their art. Little is known about this complex and ancient religion, but from Moche iconography and excavation finds, archaeologists have been able to piece together a picture. The recent discovery of human skeletons and lobster remains in a ritual context has confirmed suspicions that they practised human sacrifice – and that lobsters played a vital role in the ceremonies.

Before the sacrifice took place, a lobster would be presented to the human offering; but not, as you might suspect, as a last supper. By placing it over a steaming pot, the high priest would coax the lobster to sing. The temperature of the steam would be high enough to force air from the lobster's body in the form of song, but not so high as to cook it. Once at optimum heat, the lobster would sing an unearthly song so beautiful that the victim would become transfixed, and in a state of ecstasy give himself up for sacrifice without struggle. The sacrificial lobster, however, did not die such a peaceful death, and would be buried alive with the body of the victim.

Archaeologists also believe that lobsters sang at Moche fertility and coronation ceremonies, and that their high-pitched songs were the very first operas. Nowadays, of course, the ancient art of lobster-coaxing has been lost, but references to the lobster's superb vocal skills do surface now and again, most notably in the song 'Rock Lobster' by the B-52's.

Do hamsters get hangovers?

When a group of lively hamsters are out on the town knocking back pint after pint, drinking tequila shots off the bodies of scantily-clad strippers, they needn't worry about a fuzzy head and dodgy tummy the next day. For the humble hamster, the godforsaken hangover is a thing of the past, destined never to darken their cages again.

The hamster wheel – designed by French scientist Dr Jean-Claude Christophe Philippe – was invented to help reduce obesity in adolescent hamsters. While benefiting the lumpy youths' health, the exercise device, when used regularly before a night out, also has the bizarre side effect of hangover prevention.

The high-speed anti-clockwise movement of the wheel, generated while running, forces the eyes to repeat a fluid 'floor-to-ceiling' pattern as the wheel moves over the hamster. This stimulates verso haemophosis (inversed blood flow) which halves the dehydrating effect of alcohol and therefore eradicates any physical hangover symptoms.

When Hammy opens his little eyes after a heavy night on the lash and rolls over to be greeted by the fugly face (or arse) of a fellow furry creature, he feels as fresh as he does every other morning. And despite the stale smell of beer and cigarettes on his whiskers, and the blush-inducing memories of last night's raucous behaviour flooding back with alarming clarity, he can get on with his day as normal.

Some nightclubs have installed specially modified hamster wheels with LED lights and speaker sets to encourage clubbers to curb their hangovers whilst having a good time.

How do you hypnotise a shark?

Traditional hypnosis is lost on the ocean's most fearsome predators, as Dr Hans van Rijn discovered when he and his pocket watch were swallowed whole by a great white near South Africa. But a humble Indian fisherman one day stumbled upon a surprisingly effective method, proving there may be a way to hypnotise a shark without actually having to get into the water with it.

In 1998, Sanjay Patel was out fishing alone in a small craft just off the coast of Calcutta. As fishing can be lonely work, he'd brought along a tropical fish-shaped shower radio, which was tuned in to a station that played all his favourite Bollywood songs. Lulled into sleep by the lapping waves and the midday heat, he awoke to find his boat jammed against some rocks and rapidly sinking. Before long he was stranded, treading water in shark-infested territory.

Attracted by the vibrations created by his flailing limbs, a group of hammerhead sharks gathered and approached from all sides. And then a strange thing happened. Just as they came within striking range, they stopped dead still, and, in a trance-like state, began to rock gently from side to side in time to the music still blaring from the radio slung on a cord around Sanjay's neck. As the track picked up pace so did their movements, and they drifted into a formation which Sanjay later described as not dissimilar to that adopted by dancers in the video for 'Saajanji Ghar Aaye' from *Kuch Kuch Hota Hai*, the year's highest grossing movie.

Sanjay was able to signal to a passing boat and was luckily rescued just before his radio's battery ran out. Subsequent tests carried out on aquarium specimens have proved inconclusive, but the most encouraging results have been achieved with Bollywood classics, bhangra and drum and bass.

What would happen if you cut off a camel's hump?

In 1971 the Egyptian army published a handbook titled *Sphinx Survival IV: Back to the Pyramids*. Although it has been reprinted since with the following information withdrawn from relevant chapters (due to animal rights activists' objections), much of the material is widely considered to be accurate and essential for staying alive in harsh North African desert conditions.

Chapter 12 (Food, Drink and Mirages) focuses on the resourcefulness of the Egyptian soldiers' trusty steed, the camel, highlighting its various useful and nutritious properties, including: tail hair (which has a soothing effect when smoked); hoof shavings (which adds a kick to bland maize dishes); and camel spit (an effective cleaning fluid with a similar industrial strength to nail varnish remover).

For extreme drought conditions, often experienced during wartime exploration or undercover reconnaissance missions, the book recommends performing two hump-based procedures on your camel to provide water when supplies have dwindled. Firstly, 'hump-boring', where small incisions are made into the live camel's hump with bamboo canes or a bicycle pump and water is literally sucked up through the 'straw' device. As the hump is largely made up of cartilage, the camel allegedly feels little pain. This is not the case with the 'humpectomy', where an amputation of the hump is performed, killing the camel, to allow a group of soldiers access to the life-sustaining fluids it contains, using the hump similarly to a party punchbowl.

The sacrifice of a camel in order to save the lives of several men was deemed acceptable. Criticisms have arisen when reports were leaked that troops, with adequate access to water supplies, performed the procedure whilst at an off-duty rave, mixing the hump's water supply with whisky and coke, encouraging each other to 'down it' from the camel bowl. Further investigations indicate some owners of two-humped camels have abused the emergency water supply even more by customising the animals' storage facilities so as to create foot spas and charging other soldiers for the privilege of using them.

Are there any sticks that pose as insects?

In the depths of the Amazon jungle, where human feet seldom tread, there grows a rare and mysterious plant – the broad-leaved shape-shifter bush, or *Extralimbus insectivorus*. Many an intrepid botanist has perished in search of a specimen of this fabled species, and few have borne witness to the imitative abilities which give it its name. Most of these first-hand accounts come from the shamans of the Ubooza Ulooza tribe, who for centuries have sung around their village fires of the plant that can change its shape.

The plant is sacred to the Ubooza shamans, who keep the location of each plant a closely guarded secret – tribesmen may only see the plant by taking part in a shamanic ritual in which they must drink the potent sap of the gurouba tree and clothe themselves in the guise of a praying mantis. In 1903, the renowned explorer Sir Wally Egremont visited the Ubooza people and, after being accepted by them, was permitted to partake in the ritual. He never returned from the expedition, but fragments of his journal were later sold to a passing trader by one of the Ubooza.

This is what it said:

'... the shaman then led me to a dense part of the forest. Felt a bloody dunce in the old mantis get-up, but managed to forge ahead. And there it finally was. Not much to look at if truth be told – largely resembled oversized privet. When the moon rose I observed a peculiar phenomenon – twigs and off-shoots seemed to develop legs and became animated, swaying in the breeze in an insect-like fashion. It wasn't until a bat swooped down to grab at one of the "insects" that I noticed the jagged strips of bark along a slit on the main trunk which suddenly swung open [indecipherable text] it was over in a flash – like the poor bat had never been there... Headed back to camp for crumpets and a spot of backgammon.'

The rest of the journal was never recovered. You can view the fragments in the special collection section of the Natural History Museum, London.

Could you train a flock of oversized geese to fly passengers across the Atlantic?

Environmentalists are constantly looking for greener ways to carry out everyday tasks; wanting to fulfil the needs of modern-day society without damaging the natural world around us. After years of campaigning for the return of horse-drawn carriages to replace petrol-guzzling taxis, lobbyists finally got the go-ahead from a number of small-town councils when they suggested strapping roller skates onto the horses, as they were then able to reach a speed comparable to their motorised rivals.

The most environmentally damaging means of transportation, the airplane, has yet to be officially replaced by any other means. The closest experimentation has come to finding a viable alternative was during the Goose Bus Trials of 1999. After years of short-distance flights where a group of geese were trained to carry a platform which provided seating for multiple passengers on their backs, it was time to truly put the transport system to the test.

A large goose bus was constructed and the dummy passengers were replaced with 25 real human volunteers (with a ratio of one bird to every three humans). The flock was assembled and the route from Worthing, Sussex to Orlando, Florida was mapped out for the birds. Take-off was a little bumpy, but nothing a shot of whisky couldn't cure, and then the buses were up, up and away, on course across the Atlantic.

It wasn't until twelve hours later, when the bus touched down on American soil, that the realities of goose flights became apparent. The fact that passengers were wet, cold and dissatisfied by the in-flight entertainment could have been easily fixed with time, but it was the birds themselves who had caused the most detrimental problem. When in flight, it appeared that geese produce exorbitant amounts of foul-smelling natural gas, making the journey unbearable for passengers (two passed out from the stench). Worse still, scientists calculated that to fly the same number of passengers across the Atlantic as a 747, the amount of gas produced by the number of geese required to make the journey possible would have a greater impact on the ozone layer than the carbon emissions from a plane. The Goose Bus Programme has since been scrapped and trials are set to begin using a pedalo plane where passengers cycle their way through the skies.

Do spiders read porn?

Spiders have long lived side by side with humans, eliciting disgust and repulsion in some, admired and encouraged by others as a means of ridding their abodes of flies. But it's not just our living space that they share – they also have in common with us one of our more taboo habits. Apart from humans, spiders are the only other creature in the natural world known to create, disseminate and take sexual pleasure from pornography.

More precisely, it is the *Lecherous pervertious* species, or common bathroom spider, which has been observed to engage in this behaviour, and they do not so much 'read' porn as 'absorb' it. Unlike in humans, it is actually the female of the species who most indulges in pornographic pursuits, and it is created by the male primarily as a mating aid, but also as a means of self-preservation.

During the mating season, the male constructs an elaborate web, onto which he secretes a concoction of chemicals which contain sexual messages in a type of code. Impressed by the exertions of the male in building this bower, the female is lured into his web, where, to her surprise and pleasure, she begins to pick up the sexual code through the fibres of her legs. She's aroused into such a state of excitement that she becomes transfixed, and the male is easily able to mount her, successfully mate and, if he gets the timing right, sneak away before her pleasure fades. For, should the male be anywhere near once the mating process is over, he would serve as a handy post-coitus snack.

Scientists have not yet been able to decode the spiders' powerful secretion, but a multinational sex shop chain is already investing considerable funds into finding a means of converting it into an aphrodisiac that may be used on humans. However, initial experiments have produced some rather alarming effects in women, including increased aggression towards men, the urge to ingest flies and, in one case, the excretion of a sticky, web-like substance from the anal glands.

What would happen if you poured custard on a Jellyfish?

The classic combination of jelly and custard has long been a mainstay at children's birthday parties, but the potential effects of the yellow substance on jellyfish is a relatively new branch of research in the field of marine biology.

Though jellyfish do not possess brains or basic sensory organs, their nervous systems do enable them to detect and react to stimuli such as light, scent and dessert sauces. Although they cannot 'see' in the way we can, their ocelli (light-sensitive organs) can sense sunlight at the water's surface and so help them to distinguish between up and down. In 2002 a group of marine biologists in Grimsby, who were investigating ways of dealing with jellyfish blooms or 'outbreaks', tested the effects of a variety of substances on the organisms. The application of custard to specimens came about as an accident, when a hapless lab assistant knocked a bowl of bananas and custard into one of the experimentation tanks. The custard was drawn through the water to their jelly-like forms and once enveloped in the substance the jellyfish's ocelli were rendered useless; disorientated, they soon became entangled in each others' tentacles. Further tests with custard led the research team to conclude that it could not be used as an effective way of combating a jellyfish bloom. Leaving aside the expense and logistical nightmare of shipping large quantities of custard out to sea, the custard would not disable the creatures' stinging tentacles, which would leave a deadly mass of jellyfish-infested custard to deal with in the post-bloom-blitz clean-up operation.

However, the research did inspire one member of the team, from a small Chinese community in Grimsby, to create a new healthy snack. Jellyfish are an important source of food in Asia, where they are made edible through a lengthy process of salting and desalting. This tends to make them rather acidic and give them a crispy texture, but the marine biologist discovered that adding custard at a key stage in the procedure meant the jelly-like consistency could be maintained and the acidity was counteracted. The recipe is still being perfected, but with any luck the 'Yello-Jello Tubs' should soon be available in a delicatessen near you.

If you glued a very small wig onto a worker ant would it be accepted back into the nest or would the other ants assume it was an Elvis tribute act and kill it?

Throughout the King's reign, Elvis tribute acts were commonplace in the animal kingdom. It was rare that you would pass a badger den or beehive without being met by the sight of a platform-wearing, quiff-sporting member of the Farthing Wood fraternity, wailing along to all-time favourites 'Hound Dog' and 'Jailhouse Rock', cheered on by a group of bra-waving Elvis fans. Things in the ant world, however, were very different indeed.

In a famous televised interview with Memphis's finest, a popular TV personality likened the hip-shaker's dance moves to a man with ants in his pants. Being from simpler times, when black was black and white was white, small-minded country folk began mercilessly destroying ant colonies – gathering up hard-working ants to stuff down their trousers in an effort to recreate the famous moves of America's finest crooner. The massacre was swift and deadly, slaughtering generations of ants – including a number of important political figures and international athletes. Most shocking of all was the 1957 Antathon Championships which were held, unhappily for the ant athletes, on the playing fields of a high school during the week leading up to prom night. Schoolboys showed no mercy to the ants in their attempts to impress the girls with their dance moves, leaving bloodshed and an immense ant anti-Elvis backlash in their wake.

Years after Elvis's death, which some conspiracy theorists believe could have been caused by red ant bites (a covert attack undertaken by special forces), it is still considered bad form to mention his name in a public ant space. Whistling his songs is an arrestable offence and any ant seen wearing a white three-piece suit, fake chest hair or an Elvis wig would give grounds for other ants to attack (and kill) it without charge. Currently, these laws are not under review.

Can a leopard change his spots?

Zoologists have proved that a survival instinct is the trigger for a leopard's spots to be activated. When they're hunting a juicy steak in the Serengeti their brain kicks their polka print into action and they are able to blend in perfectly with their surroundings to sneak up on any unsuspecting antelopes.

Although many fashionistas believe leopard print to be a timeless classic, that doesn't mean the animal that has to wear it day in, day out doesn't sometimes feel like a change. For leopards living outside their natural habitats – in zoos or when holidaying in the south of France – there's no need to keep covered up in their camouflaged togs, and these big cats are often snapped sipping cocktails or strolling along the beach decked out in the finest stripes, checks and floral prints around.

Leopards have become so diverse in their ability to recreate the latest trends that they are widely considered to be the most fashionable creature on four legs and a number of big-name designers have included actual leopards in their catwalk shows alongside world-famous models. Unfortunately, due to the

Western world's obsession with the leopard's style skills, their coats have become a must-have commodity for rich fur-lovers everywhere and their numbers have dropped considerably due to poaching.

An animal sanctuary in Kenya has developed a fashion awareness school which leopards can attend once a month to determine which styles are least desirable to the public to reduce their chances of being shot for their fur. According to the latest news from South Africa's *Style It!* magazine, this season leopards will be sporting pinstripes and pastels.

Were dinosaurs religious?

A recent find in North Dakota has shaken the bedrock of palaeontology. The dig team were shocked when they uncovered the remains of a hadrosaur, or duck-billed dinosaur, with some of its skin still intact. This in itself was an unprecedented discovery, but when the palaeontologists examined the skin more closely, what they found stunned them even more. On a skin fragment taken from the hadrosaur's shoulder they could make out the distinct imprint of the sun in total eclipse. Subsequent excavations in the area unearthed further specimens, and those with their skin intact all displayed the same tattooed symbol. The sheer number of remains uncovered at the site has led palaeontologists to conclude that they have stumbled upon some sort of mass grave.

But what led this number of animals to their deaths in this spot? The fact that the remains were preserved in a tar pool has led to speculation that they were all followers of the Cult of the Eclipse, and that they committed mass suicide. Carbon dating has shown that the bones date back to 50 million BC, the exact time of their death coinciding with a total eclipse of the sun. Whether they believed the end of the world had come, or that they would gain guaranteed access to some sort of dino-heaven by taking their lives at this auspicious moment, we shall never know.

The discovery has led scientists to consider whether recent finds of 'feathered' dinosaurs in China were of a genuine new species, or whether they were merely the remains of veloceraptors who had been participating in some sort of costumed ritual dance when they died. Christian spokespeople around the world have been keen to revoke these claims, not least of all because they are worried the renewed public interest in dinosaurs might encourage Hollywood investors to fund *Jurassic Park IV*.

Do elephants ever forget?

If there was ever a place to answer this question, the annual Elephant Memory Tests would be it. The high-profile international competition was established by a Cambridge biology professor in 1882 to determine whether elephants, if placed under extreme amounts of pressure, would be able to draw on their extraordinary levels of memory, or if the competitive environment, combined with unfamiliar circumstances, would throw them off, forcing participants to forget and bow out of the tournament.

Initially set up as a scientific experiment, elephants across the globe embraced the challenge wanting to prove their worth and claim the 'Total Recall' title, and it soon became the most prestigious event on the four-legged calendar.

Lasting seven days, competitors' memories were pushed to their limits in a variety of ways from repeating number sequences to explaining soap opera storylines and performing street dance routines – all done in front of a panel of judges. There were technical failings in some of the tasks set – elephants struggled to recreate complicated culinary masterpieces even though they could verbally repeat the various stages required. But overall the mnemonic abilities of the athletes were exemplary, with tiredness being the only reason for elephants pulling out of the tournament.

The 'Tests' came into disrepute nearly a century later in 1979, when the introduction of random drug screenings revealed that over half of the registered participants tested positive for mind-enhancing substance use. They had clearly been snorting it in large quantities through their vacuum cleaner-esque trunks. It was decided that all previous champions should be stripped of their titles for fear that the drugs could have dramatically affected their performances.

While most elephants returned to a life of amateur memory testing, embarrassed by the negative press, there were some medal winners – including the great Barbar of Varanasi – who refused to let go of the dream. Barbar became obsessed with proving the power of his brain and privately took huge quantities of steroids to build up his memory muscles. His addiction resulted in severe side effects, which ironically included memory loss. He even forgot his own name, and was reduced to working as a male escort to fund his habit. Barbar died of an overdose in 1987.

Is the Easter Bunny obese?

In 1945, the British bunny situation was in a bad way. Thousands of floppy-eared, bucked-toothed rabbits had been bred to serve as suicide bombers on the front line. But without their wartime raison d'être the overcrowded rabbit farms had nowhere to send the rapidly reproducing critters and so an alternative use for the unwanted 'rabbit runners' was devised. After much debate, a select committee announced the formation of the Easter Bunny Breeding Board – a government agency responsible for the distribution of Easter-time rabbits to taxpaying families across the country.

At a time of rationing, where limited food supplies were available to the working classes, these government gifts were greatly appreciated, and usually stewed or roasted for an Easter weekend feast. But eventually food restrictions were lifted and confectioners began promoting their goods by sponsoring bunny deliveries – sending out a free bar of chocolate with each rabbit. This proved to be detrimental to the cotton-tailed critters who couldn't resist tucking in to the sweetie snacks in transit, much to the annoyance of the chocolate companies and their expectant customers.

Despite government diet recommendations and slimming classes, nothing could stop the Easter bunnies guzzling choco-treats, pushing their waistlines to the max. After years of obese generations, today's Easter bunnies have proved to be too fat for transportation services to handle and the couriers have since withdrawn from the system, despite numerous protests.

A sample from the current batch of seasonal bunnies has been sent to an Arizonian fat camp to determine whether a UK-based intensive fitness regime would be a cost-effective way of returning the much-loved tradition to the British people.

What do ostriches think about when they have their heads stuck in the sand?

The average ostrich brain is just one-eighth the size of a human brain and their cognitive abilities are restricted to essential thought processes such as working out where to find food, assessing a potential threat, and wondering just how long they'll have to keep flapping their wings before they finally take off. To put it mildly, it is unlikely that any ostrich would be eligible for Mensa membership.

However, recent studies have shown that putting their heads underground actually increases their brain power by up to ten times. Scientists aren't sure why this is, but believe it may be due to a combination of the increase in blood flow to the brain and the 'amplification' of their neural pulses by particles of sand. The research has shown that the head-burial reflex helps them to think more clearly, suggesting that their instinct to do so springs not from a desire to make themselves invisible (the common explanation for this behaviour), but from a need to calm themselves down when they're in a tight spot, for example when threatened by a predator or during an argument with a spouse, and work out how they're going to get out of it.

One drawback is, of course, that they are vulnerable to attack in this position. Another is that, since this is the only time their minds are open to contemplation of matters of a higher nature, they are prone to seize the opportunity to engage in deeply philosophical thought. When this happens they can sometimes spend hours in the pose, addressing such questions as: 'Can ostriches truly experience love, or is it all just hormones?', 'When I lift my head, will I still be me, or a different version of me?' and 'Oooh, I wonder if we should try a different shade of foliage for the nest this season?'

Why doesn't the Loch Ness Monster swim to warmer waters?

As much as we'd like to think Nessie was sticking around up north because she's raising a family, or loves the local people, the fact is it all comes down to money. Nowhere else will pay her as well. As one of the world's only remaining animal anomalies, this dino-descendant can command substantial royalties from any photographs taken (fake and real), sighting stories and all merchandise and subsequent media (even films) that trade on her name.

So you'd think that after 300 years of working in the business she'd be able to get pretty much whatever she wanted – including a home-relocation to somewhere a little warmer where she could eventually retire and live out her days in the sunshine. Unfortunately for old Ness there are no bodies of water in the world that can afford to take the risk of accommodating her in the vague hope that people will believe she's moved. Nessie will only be able to maintain the luxurious, party-animal lifestyle (and fruit-machine addiction) to which she has become accustomed if the government or private owner of her prospective home can guarantee a millionaire's income. The water-monster's desired contract states that if her host fails to raise the money through tourism, they must cough it up themselves – and these are sums no individual, or even country, can afford. Much of the Scottish mythology surrounding Loch Ness brings thousands of people to the area every year desperate to catch a glimpse of her so it's not surprising that no one else is prepared to take the gamble.

With two reported children and another on the way, it looks like Nessie will have to make do with her chilly residence until she decides to throw in the towel (or when she's earned enough money). It's not all bad, though; every winter, when the tourist season has died down, she takes a three-month trip to the Seychelles to visit her husband and the kids who moved out there a few years ago and tops up her tan so she's always looking her best when she returns to Scotland for the summer.

IN MY TUMMY

Have you seen the Muffin Man?

We have never personally seen the Muffin Man (Old Muffy), what with him having died in 1899, although it is said that his ghost haunts London's Drury Lane seeking revenge on the man who killed him.

Many people believe the original Muffin Man to have worked on Cherry Lane (a popular prostitute hang-out), but this is a common mistake. Old Muffy baked traditional English muffins every morning and went door to door down Drury Lane selling his wares to the good folk of Victorian London. For years he had been the most popular baker in town, and despite his good fortune and comfortable lifestyle he always made a point of delivering the muffins himself and chatting to his customers as he went. In 1898, after nearly thirty years of 'muffing', a new muffin maker came on the scene. Little Muff, a younger, more attractive baker, set up shop on Cherry Lane and started selling the American-style muffins we're familiar with today to the brothel owners and prostitutes in the area in return for sexual favours. Soon the great and the good of London were travelling to the dodgy street to pick up blueberry tops, chocolate chip and apricot jam muffins for twice the price of Old Muffy's original cakes. He was distraught, and as his business began to fail he turned to drink. Early one morning, Old Muffy found himself drunkenly staggering down Cherry Lane when he came across Little Muff setting up shop for the day. A fight ensued and Little Muff, being stronger and more familiar with street fighting techniques, got Old Muffy in a headlock and shoved him into his bread oven. Because of all the hoo-ha going on with Jack the Ripper's latest killing spree, Old Muffy's death was pushed down the list of important things for London's police squad to investigate. It was only months later when they finally realised Little Muff was responsible that they tried to track him down to arrest him. Unfortunately, the cunning baker had fled Cherry Lane for the Americas, where he took his recipes and continued to make his fortune. He told everyone that he was London's notorious Muffin Man from Cherry Lane (hence the confusion with the nursery rhyme), and soon became a huge success.

And now all that is left of Old Muffy's legacy is a small plaque on Cherry Lane that police erected during the hunt for his killer which reads: 'Have you seen the Muffin Man? Wanted for the death of the original Muffin Man who lived on Drury Lane.'

How fast can a runner bean run?

The humble runner bean is known for its hardy nature and high nutritional yield relative to the amount of attention it requires, making it a popular choice in vegetable gardens and allotments, and especially with novice gardeners. It is a common misconception that its name comes from the plant's tendency to 'run' its tendrils along bamboo canes or other supports and so grow upwards. In fact, the true origins of its name lie in a far more surprising behavioural pattern that makes the runner bean unique in the vegetable kingdom.

Long before the first gardener came along and used his green fingers to coax the plant to grow up and away from the ground, runner beans were preyed upon by a particularly vicious type of rodent: the round-bottomed pulse rat. This repulsive creature, notorious for its putrid odour, would stuff runner beans into its mouth whole, churn them up and spit out the stringy skins, leaving a wake of destruction in its path.

But not if the beans could get away first. Once alerted to the presence of the pulse rat by the pungent smells emitted from its gassy behind, the canny beans would detach themselves from the plant and sprint away, sometimes reaching speeds of up to ten miles an hour. Which, if you take into account the size of the bean and the fact that it has no eyes to see where it's going, is pretty impressive.

Nowadays, due to the extinction of the pulse rat, runner beans very rarely exhibit this behaviour. But next time you're in your dad's veggie patch, if you happen to break wind, you might just be greeted with the sight of his prize crop streaking away over the garden fence…

What is cottage cheese?

Many things are compared to cottage cheese – babies' sick, regular sick, that weird pollution crap you get floating on the top of dirty streams… but despite buying it in those cute little tubs at their local supermarket, few people actually know where it comes from or what it is.

Try not to be too alarmed, but it's not cheese. It was not always sold as cheese but when the original producers found no one was taking home their cheesy flavoured product when it was called by its real name, they settled on this as a suitable alternative. Cottage cheese was discovered by a couple living in a Devonshire thatched cottage. One year they smelt a pungent cheese smell coming from their roof and decided to investigate. What they discovered were the recently hatched babies of the silver hay bug which had infested their thatch. They called in an exterminator, but were taken aback when they noticed their cat gobbling up the newborns and licking his lips. Knowing that Whiskers was very particular about his diet they decided to see what all the fuss was about and swallowed a couple of the little blighters themselves. They too were pleasantly surprised, although they found the bugs a little bitter and quite wriggly. After setting up their own silver hay critter farm and months of experimentation, they discovered that by mixing the offspring with a milky sour cream and refrigerating the result (causing the hatchlings to become comatose) they had created themselves a new snack product that worked a treat on jacket potatoes, with salads and on toast, and after the label change (it used to be called Creamy Bug Babies) the public would be none the wiser.

Just don't leave it out of the fridge for too long: the babies do eventually wake up.

Why do People eat Popcorn at the Movies?

It is a sad fact that hordes of cinema-goers around the world mindlessly stuff popcorn into their mouths without comprehending the true significance of their actions. In the 1920s, when films first hit the big screen, not all towns could afford to build cinemas at first, and so the first 'blockbusters' were screened in makeshift cinemas set up in communal spaces such as town halls, school gymnasiums and barns. That was until disaster struck in one barn in Carmel, Indiana.

Farmer Cochran was very pleased to have managed to get that summer's harvest of corn neatly stowed away underneath his barn-cum-cinema's seating area in time for the release of the latest Chaplin flick. As the audience chuckled away at the diminutive entertainer's antics, heat transference from the old-fashioned projector started a small hay fire at the back of the barn. The heat caused the corn to 'pop', the crackling sounds alerting the ushers that something was wrong. On discovering the fire they turned to evacuate the barn, but it was too late: when the audience tried to escape they found themselves blocked in by a mountain of freshly popped corn pushing its way up through the floorboards.

According to post-mortem evidence the movie-lovers closest to the popcorn wall began munching away in a belly-busting attempt to free themselves from the barn, with little regard for whether it was salty, sweet or toffee-coated. Not one of the cinema-goers survived, but some of the popped corn did escape the blaze, sent sky high by the final explosion which destroyed the barn, and was unwittingly sampled by the crowd who had gathered to marvel in open-mouthed wonder at the spectacle.

Popcorn was made and passed around at the memorial service, and was served at cinemas from that day forward as a sign of respect to those who lost their lives and to act as a reminder of the dangers of fire, with all proceeds going to the families of the victims. So, next time you're at the cinema and tucking in to a bucket of sweet 'n' salty (or flicking it at the people kissing on the row in front), take a moment to pause and reflect on the loss of human life that brought this crunchy treat into your lap.

Marmite – is it true that you either love it or hate it?

The truth is that everybody loves Marmite. The human body is predisposed to 'love' foods that are good for it, and as a ready source of yeast and vitamin B, what's not to like? But thanks to a psychic experiment that got out of hand, there are some people out there who are convinced they 'hate' Marmite.

In the post-war ration period, Marmite became a top item on everyone's shopping list thanks to its versatility: it could be added to watery vegetable soup for an extra kick of flavour, diluted in hot water as a warming winter drink, or spread thinly over toast to disguise the taste of mouldy bread. The yeast extract spread continued to be popular well into the 1950s, until a leading competitor threw a spanner in the works.

Edward Scrimp, the managing director of the company which produced Yeasty-Feast spread, decided to sabotage Marmite's success and sent a psychic spy over to Marmite headquarters to plant subliminal messages in the new logo during a major rebranding operation. The lettering of the label, which reads 'MARMITE' and then 'YEAST EXTRACT' underneath, was rearranged in such a way that the subconscious mind would initially pick out only the following letters: 'ARM EXTRACT'. Suffice to say, the notion of spreading liquidised biceps or puréed elbow on one's toast is enough to put most people off their food.

What Scrimp didn't count on was the fact that this type of messaging only works on a small percentage of people, so, whilst noticeable, the drop in sales wasn't significant enough to give Yeasty-Feast the edge in the market, and they soon went out of business. (Their sales figures weren't helped by a Sunday tabloid scandal involving MD Edward Scrimp, a tub of chocolate spread – not Yeasty-Feast – and a few low-class hookers.)

By the time Marmite discovered what had happened it was too far down the line to change the logo, which had by that stage become an iconic household brand. In any case, Marmite was so massively popular by then that a few million people thinking they hated the stuff didn't make much of a dent in profit. It's just a shame that, to this day, some people are missing out on this tasty, nutritious treat.

Do superheroes like cheese?

Superheroes are not like normal people. They fight evil, they wear Lycra, they always give up their seats for the elderly... And their attitude towards cheese is no exception. Whereas some humans cannot stand the stench of a wheel of Stilton or the taste of a fine chunk of Cheshire, *all* superheroes love cheese.

The superhero appetite for this dairy delight was reaching such a height last year that masked mistress Mighty Nova, whose superpower allows her to turn humans into mice, founded a dairy products appreciation society to invite fellow superpowered types to meet up, taste and chat about cheese.

Soon celebrity heroes including Dubious, Dragon Diva, Punchface, Strikeforce and White Dinosaur were meeting up once a week to sample the latest lactose treats from up and down the country. White Dinosaur, being the eldest amongst them, commanded a certain amount of respect. He declared that they should put their cheese-chewing skills to use and begin production on a cheese never before consumed by common folk, as they were, after all, *not* common folk.

His loyal sidekick, Dubious, who was great with a big stick (and, despite being lactose intolerant, enjoyed a fine piece of Brie), was always a bit cautious, ever since he invested in White Dinosaur's dotcom bra-selling idea. But after a few glasses of claret and a tickle from Punchface, he was won round and the Panda Cheese™ Company was born.

Rare, grey in colour, and with a distinct woody aftertaste, Panda Cheese™ is thought to be one of the most daring new cheeses to come on the market since the slug cream cheese fad of 1997. With a photograph of PCC lovelies – Mighty Nova, Dragon Diva and new recruit Herminator – hugging a panda from their Chengdu panda dairy on the cover of each packet, it's been flying off the shelves.

In their fight to provide the country with an exciting new cheese, the PCC has come to realise its immense heroic ability, and has set up a crime-fighting superhero branch called The League of Titans (*tit-an* is the Chengdu dialect Mandarin word for cheese).

Where does mayonnaise really come from?

Let's face it: the snack industry wouldn't be what it is today without mayonnaise. Pre-packed sandwiches would be unlubricated and dry, chips and dips would be a limited affair, and the Dutch would be at a complete loss as to what to put on their fries. All of which adds up to a pretty good case for keeping the true source of mayonnaise from the general public. Though the substance is completely harmless to the human digestive system, most people wouldn't be able to stomach it if they knew where it really came from. Coleslaw addicts: look away now.

In the late 1800s, as the global colonial scramble reached fever pitch, explorers from the Western world were discovering new flora and fauna that defied the imagination and, in some cases, classification. So it was with the mysterious sea cucumber: was it a water-grown salad vegetable? Was it a creature without features? Or was it some poor sea mammal's dismembered member? The Dutch explorer and wannabe zoologist Van der Vank was determined to find out, and so he shipped a batch of healthy specimens back to the Netherlands for observation.

After months of experimentation, and having exhausted the possibilities of classification within the known animal kingdom, Van der Vank decided that it was indeed a vegetable and bravely served one up for tasting with Sunday brunch. It was as he attempted to get a grip on the flaccid and slimy cucumber to slice it up that the creature began to slide uncontrollably back and forth in his hand, triggering its unique defence mechanism and spurting a creamy, viscous substance over his side order of fries. On sampling them Van der Vank declared that the fries tasted 'infinitely better' and, though at first reluctant, the other diners couldn't help but agree.

It wasn't long before Van der Vank's fellow countrymen realised the gastronomical possibilities of his discovery and, in order to streamline the extraction process, developed a piston action machine (similar to a dairy milking machine, but with a jerkier action) that manufacturers still use in modern mayonnaise farms. They cunningly concealed the true source of the versatile condiment, selling it under the label of 'a subtle blend of egg yolks and oil, whipped to perfection for your delectation', and the facade has been maintained to this very day.

Could you turn a pumpkin into a carriage?

When Cinderella's godmother showed up in the nick of time to transform the unwashed scullery maid into a sparkling lady fit for the ball, she didn't forget that a fairy-tale princess can hardly show up at a royal event without a glittery carriage, and so she turned to the nearest home-grown vegetable and instantly a plump orange pumpkin was transformed into a fancy horse-drawn taxi. Everyone loves the story, but is there any truth in it?

One Californian daddy's girl refused to take no for an answer. She believed that with the right amount of whining, sulking and sucking up, anything was possible. Two years before her high-school prom, she told her father that she wanted to show up to the party in a carriage which had been magically created from a pumpkin. Not wanting to shatter his only daughter's dreams he set about hiring the help of Idaho's most prestigious pumpkin farmer, and paid him well to produce a batch of the largest pumpkins on record – with the help of some hard-core veggie steroids.

After two years of growing, finally a pumpkin that was large enough was carved by a pair of Swedish ice sculptors, who slaved away for a month to create a truly magical-looking carriage, complete with rotating wheels, door and a surround-sound music system. Unfortunately, by the time the prom came round and the carriage was ready to be drawn by two white ponies down the Orange County highway to the princess's prom night, the remaining flesh of the pumpkin (hidden by the upholstery) began to rot and a putrid smell oozed from the carriage.

The high-schooler was distraught, but her father managed to console her. He said that, just like in the fairy tale, if she was to go in a pumpkin carriage she'd have to get back for a twelve o'clock curfew. It was a tough decision, but she settled for a stretch limo, which meant she could stay out until two.

How many trees does it take to make a Black Forest gateau?

The chocolate-and-cherry-flavoured cream-topped cakes you will find in the frozen food section of your local supermarket or in the fancy spinning dessert cabinet of a restaurant bear little resemblance to the original Black Forest gateau, created at the command of Prince Wolfgang III in 1823.

In his long and unsuccessful search for a bride, Wolfgang had observed one common trait in all the women he had met: a certain weakness for cake, especially of the chocolate variety. And so, when his father announced that the beautiful Princess of Bavaria would be attending the Royal Autumn Ball, he set out to create a cake of proportions beyond any female's wildest dessert fantasies.

Standing at twenty feet high and fifty feet across, it would be made up of ten layers of chocolate cake and contain seventy gallons of whipped cream, twenty gallons of cherry jam, and topped with a ton of chocolate sprinkles. Every baker, dairy cow herd and cherry orchard in the land was commandeered for the creation of the project and an enormous kiln was erected in which to cook the gargantuan cake. No less than 2,000 trees from the nearby Black Forest were felled to feed the flames.

The dessert was the *pièce de résistance* at the royal feast and the princess was suitably impressed. However, in accepting the honour of cutting the first slice she had bitten off more than she could chew, so to speak. As she began to slice down through the cake, she set off violent vibrations that shook its fragile infrastructure, causing first an avalanche of cream from the cake's northernmost plateau followed by the unstoppable descent of each layer to the floor. Fifty courtiers and aristocrats were killed, including the princess. The prince survived with only a mild lactose reaction, but never ate cake again.

Modern anti-deforestation laws mean that it would now be strictly forbidden to attempt to follow the original recipe, but using one pine tree felled from a sustainable forest you could generate enough heat to bake a miniature one-foot-tall tribute, which should be enough to impress on a first date.

Are there any foods that can make me lighter?

Even though many diet foods make wild promises proclaiming their weight-loss, mind-enhancing and energising properties, there are strict regulations over what manufacturers are allowed to put on packaging. Just make sure you read the small print…

One of the most confusing words that makes its way onto labels is 'light'. Nowadays we have the choice of light drinks, dairy products and savoury snacks, and most people opt for these when they're trying to cut down on calories in a bid to battle the bulge. Given that most people don't read the tiny disclaimers and content jargon when they're shopping, these 'light eaters' would be surprised by what they'd discover if they did.

'Light' is one of the FSA (Food Standards Agency)'s most controversial words as, in reality, it doesn't mean that the food is a healthy option but that by eating it the consumer will temporarily be lighter in weight. In order to achieve 'light' status, foods usually contain an additive called prolebersene, which causes the blood cells to take in more oxygen and absorb any helium found naturally in the air, and in a sense become more buoyant. A high dosage of the additive (much higher than the amount found in any light foods) could cause the eater to lift off their feet – but their heart would probably stop because of the lightness of the blood moving through it before they reached the 'take-off' stage.

'Light' snacks make the eater feel lighter, and for a short time they will actually be lighter until the blood regulates itself, so they therefore feel that the diet of light snacks is working when, in fact, they are poisoning their blood and eating normal amounts of salts and fats. To avoid confusion, and because they cannot use the word 'light', some companies have opted for the word 'lite' instead, which is often used to describe a food lower in fats or sugars.

Why are Pineapples so spiky?

Fruit are emotional beings and none more so than the prickly pineapple. You might think that its spiky exterior is developed as a means of protecting itself against marauding monkeys, but with enough determination any sweet-toothed creature can manage to split the fruit in half to get at its juicy insides. No, the spiky exterior of the pineapple fruit is in fact a reflection of the emotional turmoil it goes through as it ripens.

The process of developing from a seed into a fully formed fruit is fuelled by growth hormones, which are not without their side effects. Just as teenagers are prone to acne, young pineapples manifest lumps and bumps on their outer layer of skin. The pressure of trying to outgrow their peer pineapples leads to enormous frustration for the fruit, and this sense of irritation is vividly demonstrated by the spikes which push their way out through their skin. Finally, their aggression towards each other causes hard green spines to sprout out of their heads – the equivalent of a human having a permanent bad hair day.

People who eat large quantities of pineapple have been observed to experience similar emotional effects, their mood becoming predominantly sullen. Pineapple lovers are more prone to enjoy the wailings of emo music, read Nietzsche and sound like they're in an episode of *The O.C.* Conversely, eating a lot of bananas tends to make people feel warm and smiley. Famous banana addicts include Tony Blair (since leaving office), Dawn French and smiley, smiley Carol Smillie. All of which goes to show what you feel on the inside affects the way you are seen by others. No one has ever managed to eat enough coconuts to be able to empathise with what makes them come over all hard and hairy, but many young men have tried.

A man cannot live on bread alone, but could he live on jam alone?

In 1893, a ship carrying supplies for a cricket tournament in the Bahamas was wrecked at sea. Almost all the crew and cargo was wiped out, except for two men who floated to shore on a raft fashioned out of three giant loaves of bread, and one man who drifted to safety astride a barrel of raspberry jam. There was nothing to be done but to sit out a week until the next scheduled cargo ship passed by and rescued them.

Now, it would be no bad thing to be stranded on a desert island if you had the good fortune to be left with the ingredients for a week's worth of tasty afternoon snacks, but unfortunately the man with the sandwich filling was in a bit of a sticky situation, having been washed up on a different island to his fellow survivors, with 600 feet of shark-infested waters separating them.

The men with the bread fared well in the first couple of days, having a good source of carbohydrate to keep them going. By mid-week, however, they were experiencing extreme bloating from the amount of wheat they had consumed, and the bread had begun to go stale. By day six they were completely dehydrated, with nothing to drink and only dry bread to chew on, and by day seven they were barely alive – bedraggled shadows of themselves, with surprisingly stylish stubble growth.

The man with the jam, however, did unexpectedly well. The first two days were a whirl of sugar highs and lows, battles with nausea and extreme constipation as he got to grips with his new sugar-loaded diet. By day three he had stabilised, though, and by nightfall he managed to pass his first stool on the island. Being rich in raspberry seeds, his fruity-smelling faeces attracted small lizards, which he was able to trap and kill as a source of protein. He spent the rest of the week experimenting with ways to cook the meat in the jam and was able to greet his rescuers with a gourmet feast of 'lizard confit' when they arrived at the end of the week.

Of course, had the situation continued for an indefinite amount of time, he would undoubtedly have lost most of his teeth to tooth decay and would have struggled to chew the leathery lizard meat. However, you can't help but admit he had a much better time of it than his doughy friends, and this is in fact where the expression 'jammy' (used in the sense of 'lucky' or 'fortunate') originally came from.

How easy is it to slip on a banana skin?

It's one of the oldest visual gags going. Man walks down a street and slips on a banana skin that just happens to be sitting there. But what are the chances of that actually happening? How likely is it you wouldn't see the banana? Would an empty skin on a concrete pavement really be that slippery? And if you did slip, would you recreate a comedy fall to rival the likes of Laurel and Hardy, and survive with no serious injuries?

Cambridge University has spent the last three years conducting a study to determine the answers to these questions. They found that on average, in the UK, one in every 25 people has slipped on a banana skin at some point. Banana skins are the most commonly discarded fruit peel, and after crisp packets, drinks cans and chewing gum the fourth most likely type of rubbish to be found on the street. They carried out 30,000 case studies with banana skins in various states of decay on various pavement surfaces in different light conditions. Their results found, rather surprisingly, that under moderate daylight, on a tarmac surface less than 2.5 metres wide, with a banana peel over one day old (dependent on whether it had rained that day) someone over six foot is highly likely to slip over and cause themselves serious injuries.

The other conclusions drawn from the study formed the basis of a new public safety act issued to local councils. Amid fears of council-operated street clean-up teams being sued for negligence, soon new 'Pick Up Your Skin' posters will be going up in Harrow, Bromley and Helensburgh to 'a-peel' to the rubbish-droppers. If it's successful in reducing the number of peels left on our pavements, we'll soon see a nationwide campaign to keep Britain's streets peel-free.

What will they do when the treacle mines run dry?

This is a question that has been worrying scientists for some time, for unlike other fossil fuels, there is no viable substitute for treacle. Cars can run on electricity instead of petrol, wind turbines can be used to create electricity instead of burning coal, and your house can be heated with solar panels rather than gas, but nothing can give the essential flavour to a treacle tart or treacle toffee but the black stuff itself.

Molasses, from which treacle is made, was formed millions of years ago when sugar deposits were laid down by fruit which had fallen from trees and been gradually covered by layers of leaves and then soil. The gloopy black substance is extracted from 'molasses veins' by treacle miners. This is a highly hazardous way to earn a living; many a treacle miner has met a sticky end when molasses has come surging out of the rock face at high pressure.

Since its discovery in the seventeenth century, the world's treacle resources have been steadily depleted. We are now facing the situation where we probably have three years at the most before supplies run out. Given this crisis, plans are in motion to ration the substance, which means we can expect a sudden rise in treacle prices in the coming months.

Admittedly, for most people there isn't any cause for real panic. The majority of customers will be happy to opt for syrup instead of treacle tart, or liquorice instead of treacle toffee. But for treacle addicts and, more importantly, sufferers of acute epidermic anaemia, the future looks very bleak indeed. Patients who have this rare disease can only absorb iron into their bloodstream through their skin. So far, the only effective means of administering this essential nutrient to sufferers is through treacle baths. Medical researchers are now experimenting with Guinness showers, black pudding compresses and spinach lotion in an effort to find an alternative method of treatment.

What makes a fruit a fruit?

For over a century, the world has felt quite comfortable with its laymen's definition of a fruit and how it differs from a vegetable. The former hangs from trees or bushes, the latter grows inside the earth. But there are still areas of discrepancy. The common tomato (a popular salad vegetable, usually eaten as a savoury accompaniment) is technically a fruit, as is the blue-top carrot (an Icelandic variety which grows out of the earth on a wild, truncated bush). We're probably all in agreement that whichever way we want to look at it, potatoes, rice and Shredded Wheat are not part of our five-a-day (unless you put a banana on your cereal – with lashings of ice-cold milk).

As the story goes, a long, long time ago, a posh bloke called Lord Wilkins (or Jonathan to his close friends) was hanging out on his large country estate and had taken up a popular Georgian hobby – vegetable presentation. Much like today's popular village vegetable-growing competitions, Jonathan and his friends would get dressed up in their finery and parade their various food produce to each other in an entertaining fashion. At the time, all non-animal food items (anything naturally grown) were known as vegetables, but the Lord was not happy. When explorers returned from India with large round oranges (unlike anything naturally grown in the UK) he began rolling them through croquet hoops as part of his presentation strategy, earning him respect and high marks from his fellow vegetable presenters. As the orange passed through the hoop he would shout out, 'Through it!' in a high-pitched squeal of delight. As time progressed other presenters would bring with them more exotic and round-shaped items to present and roll through the hoops, and these vegetables later became known as 'through-its'. Because the vegetable market-sellers' take on the term usually involved dropping the 'th' sound in favour of 'f', all round-shaped foods became known as 'fru-its'.

The pastime has long-since been forgotten and is only practised as a May Day tradition on some estates, so the criteria for a fruit (that it is round and fits through a croquet hoop) have been forgotten with it, meaning bananas, pineapples and large watermelons all now belong to the 'through-it' family.

Are there any foods that can double up as weapons?

In this day and age, when street crime is rife and a mugger could be lurking around every corner, it's only natural that you would want to protect yourself. And, since it is illegal to carry knives, baseball bats or other traditional weapons as a means of defence, the time has come to get creative. With the right handbag- or pocket-sized snack, you can stay on the right side of the law and give street criminals more than they bargained for.

We may all laugh at the French for going about their business with a stick of bread wedged in their armpit, but a well-aimed blow to the head with a baguette can knock an assailant for six, giving you ample time to make your getaway. Just make sure your bready club is at least three days old, otherwise you will merely anger your attacker and be left holding a floppy stick. Not a good look.

Another more discreet means of defence is sherbet. A handful of this stuff in the eyes is temporarily blinding – by the time your attacker has blinked their way out of the confectionary haze, you'll have made good your escape. Other useful sweets to carry about your person are liquorice whips, gobstoppers and candy canes. However, the use of these will involve some close combat with the assailant, and are not recommended unless you have at least some previous experience of one-to-one fighting.

And last but not least, nothing can compare with the searing pain of being struck full in the eye with a frozen rum ball. These chocolate-vermicelli-coated, rum-soaked balls of stodgy cake are only to be found in the very best old-fashioned bakeries, but you can easily make them at home. They are most effective when frozen solid, so if you're taking one out with you, you may want to keep it in a freezer bag to prevent any leakage when the ball begins to defrost. The freezer bag will also double up as a handy swinging aid, allowing you to whack your attacker in the eye and then retract your rum-ball for another tasty uppercut wallop to the nose if required.

If I can't have my cake and eat it, what am I supposed to do with it?

There are a number of interesting things you can do with cake (depending on the type of cake you've got) that doesn't involve eating it. Try some of the following suggestions and see how they compare to biting into that sweet fluffy sponge and sugary icing.

1) Still life painting is a great way to show someone you're cultured and sophisticated. Put the cake on an antique table surrounded by some interesting artefacts (perhaps a scroll and a bronze bust of a famous explorer) and get your watercolours out. If you're proud of your work, give it to a loved one as a gift, sell it on eBay or give it a fitting name, such as *Cake Uneaten No. 7* and submit it as your entry for the Turner Prize.

2) Celebrity fad dieting – some involve cabbage soup, others boiled eggs, and some even mean you get to carry around your lunch in your handbag (the baby food diet), but the chocolate cake diet is the one to try out. Stand in your kitchen staring at your big, fat chocolate cake. Stare at it for thirty minutes and then leave the

room. This staring process will psychologically trick you, allegedly, into thinking you've eaten an entire chocolate cake, and you can get on with your day without getting the munchies.

3) If it's good enough for clowns and the cast of *Bugsy Malone* then it's good enough for you. Stop whingeing about not eating your cake and get a bunch of your mates together for a mammoth food fight. We recommend anything with lots of buttercream and a few little fairy cakes for good projectile capabilities.

4) Dress up in your finest Victorian garb and make your way down to a quaint village fete. Your costume will be welcomed by locals and foreign tourists alike, as will the cakes you bring along to sell on your stall. Make sure you label up your wares in the old money (you know, guineas and shillings) for that authentic cake sale vibe.

5) Sometimes the simplest things are the best. The jilted Miss Haversham of *Great Expectations* fame showed us how it's done by leaving a wedding cake to rot on her dining room table. Make sure you take photos as your cake decays to capture the various stages of decomposition. NB: Fruit cake will take a while to perish – try fruit-topped cheesecake for a quick rotting fix.

AROUND THE WORLD IN 18 QUESTIONS

In the event of a zombie apocalypse, where would be the safest place to run to?

As we all know, civilisation is fragile and liable to be overturned by chaos when faced with a threat such as a plague of flesh-eating zombies. In most countries, an outbreak would be greeted by initial disbelief and inaction from the government, followed by ineffective measures that would lead to the nationwide collapse of large-scale organisations. But not so in the mountains of Transylvania, for the people of these communities have been dealing with the undead for quite some time.

Long ago, when the Transylvanians lived under the shadow of Vlad the Impaler, they learned that the secret to dealing with the undead lay in knowing their weaknesses and being prepared. And so, through judicious use of garlic, holy water and wooden stakes they have been able to manage their vampire problem and keep it under control to this day.

There is no doubt that these pragmatic and resolute people would react in a similar way on hearing the news of a zombie outbreak elsewhere in the world. By the time the plague had reached their neighbouring regions, they would have readied themselves for a siege at the nearest castle and set landmines in the peripheral woods in order to disable and slow down as many of the oncoming hordes as possible. Equipped with weapons and a vantage point, it would just be a matter of picking the remaining zombies off as they filtered through with a shot to the head.

Were you to find yourself in a pocket of survivors, your surest chance of staying alive would be to find a way of joining the Transylvanians in their safe haven. However, even if you did make it there without being attacked by a zombie, stepping on a landmine or being picked off by any thirsty vampires that might still be flying around, your biggest challenge would be in being accepted into the community, for Transylvanians are notoriously wary of outsiders.

Why do the French eat frogs' legs?

This is something which everyone wonders about, but few dare to ask out loud. The French are a culturally advanced people, who do everything with a certain grace and *je ne sais quoi*. And, of course, they have a reputation for the most exquisite cuisine on the planet. But their predilection for frogs' legs has less to do with their culinary expertise and more to do with their Gallic sense of pride.

Way back in 1685, at the height of Louis XIV's reign, France suffered the worst summer on record and Louis had recently moved into his brand new pad – the Château de Versailles. Many of the low-lying regions were devastated by floods and the death toll amongst the peasants was high. Worse than this, the nation was hampered by a plague of frogs, which were flourishing in the wet and warm conditions, keeping everyone up at night with their incessant croaking.

As you may imagine, Louis XIV had quite a problem on his hands: since a round of croquet or hunting on his new estate was out of the question, his courtiers were bored and he needed to do something about it, fast. And so, after racking his brains as to what indoor activity he could organise to amuse them, he came up with the idea of a national culinary competition. Top chefs from every region in France were summoned to the palace and a banquet to end all banquets was prepared. With each region's chef preparing a course to impress the king, the meal went on for days and was a resounding success, with every delicacy from foie gras to quail eggs being served.

Back in the kitchens, though, it was a very different story. The extreme heat generated by all the cooking meant that the chefs had to open the kitchen door to get some air in, and with it came an army of frogs, attracted by the humid conditions within. They were everywhere: shimmying up and down the ladle handles, squatting on the giant cress leaves in the vats of soup and doing the leapfrog across the chopping boards.

When it came to the chef from Reims's turn to cook, things had reached boiling point. As he struggled to prepare his complicated dish in cramped, hot conditions, batting off frogs left, right and centre, he finally lost it and, with an almighty cry of *'Putains de grenouilles!'*, brought his cleaver down on an unfortunate frog, severing it in half at the waist. The other chefs immediately followed suit, seizing on this very effective means of disabling the hopping creatures, and carnage ensued.

Somehow, in all the confusion, disembodied pairs of legs managed to end up in the Reims dishes and no one had time to warn the waiting staff before they took them out. By the time they realised it was too late – the course had been served and the courtiers waited expectantly for the king to take the first taste. Louis, who by the thirty-second course, had had more than a few to drink, declared that they were delicious and so all the other courtiers tucked in. No one would dare to contradict the king, and the chefs didn't want to risk the nation's culinary reputation by letting the truth out, and so the dish was declared a national delicacy. And that is why it is eaten proudly by the French unto this very day, despite the fact that frogs' legs are pretty bony and greasy and taste a bit like malnourished chicken.

Under Lapland's laws do Santa's elves get paid holidays?

Following years of bad press in the 1800s, Christmas HQ decided that the public image of Santa's elves was an embarrassment to the whole institution, and that something had to be done. The problem was that despite there being thousands of elves living in remote areas all over the world, the only ones humans heard about were Santa's. And everyone knows that Santa's elves are the criminal masterminds of elf society.

Before Santa became such an important part of the festive season for so many children around the globe, he worked part-time as a probation officer, taking in naughty elves who had recently spent time in the slammer and setting them to work feeding his growing collection of reindeer and generally keeping his hundred-acre Lapland estate in good working order. He used to make the toys he handed out to well-behaved Dutch children himself and would deliver them while on his whistle-stop tour of central Europe at Christmas when he visited his family.

But then word of Santa's generosity began to spread, and he couldn't cope with the demand. This coincided with a crime wave in elfdom due to the rise of a mafioso family, and the prison system soon began to buckle. Impressed by the work Santa was doing, the probationary service started sending him more and more elves, until he had enough to set up the toymaking workshop we know of today.

When word got out that criminals were responsible for the production of Christmas toys, children were taught to despise Santa's little helpers and, for a while, it looked like Christmas was on the blink. But thanks to a startling Victorian PR campaign, and the introduction of a successful rehabilitation programme, introduced by Christmas Inc., Santa's elves soon became acceptable, well-behaved members of society – there have been a few hiccups along the way, including the Scrabble Scam of 1994, but nothing that's put the public at risk.

Although no wages are ever given to the mini toymakers (their bed and board is covered by profits made from fairy lights) they are given holiday time for good behaviour, typically in January before the workload begins. Most elves tend to vacation in Haiti where their miniature status is lauded and they are treated like gods.

What happened to the Sphinx's nose?

In the eighteenth century, the world was terrorised by a series of bizarre and disturbing acts of art crime. The cultural community watched in horror as a list of mysterious disappearances grew: the *Mona Lisa*'s smile, the *Venus de Milo*'s arms, the *Pietà*'s right big toe… Was this the work of some crazed human body part fetishist, or simply an elaborate prank?

When the sun rose on 17 January 1751 to reveal that the Sphinx's nose had been picked, a small group of Parisian Renaissance scholars decided that enough was enough and launched an investigation to get to the bottom of things, before the thieves had the chance to get their hands on the bottoms of any famous things. What they found was even more perplexing than the disappearances themselves.

By plotting the locations of the thefts on a map, the team distinguished a pattern which pointed to Switzerland as the culprit's likely base. A clairvoyant was able to determine that the suspect was more than likely a middle-aged, white Caucasian male, an outcast from society who acted alone, although how he managed to swipe the Sphinx's massive conk unaided remained unclear. One thing was certain, though: he lived next to a large body of water, and so the detectives took their search to the banks of Lake Geneva.

There they stumbled quite by chance upon a strange lair in which they found the missing artefacts arranged in some sort of experiment. The only explanation apparent to the team was that the thief was trying to create some sort of uber-art being, the pinnacle of artistic expression combined into one human form. But could the composite parts ever have formed a beautiful being as a whole, and if so, then why the big nose? But the team didn't have time to ponder the whys and wherefores – they needed to get the artefacts safely out of there before the art-crazed nutter returned. But just as they were about to heave the nose onto their shoulders, they heard heavy footsteps outside and were forced to flee, leaving the Sphinx's schnoz where it lay and dropping a pair of arms and an assortment of different sized male genitalia on their way out.

When they returned to the site the lair had been cleared out and the nose had vanished: where it went, no one knows. Mary Shelley is said to have been so inspired by the incident that she wrote *Frankenstein*, but she had to make significant revisions when her editor told her that the story lacked credibility and the title *The Monster with the Big Nose* just wouldn't sell.

In Austria, are the hills really alive with the sound of Music?

Next time you're itching to get away and the usual holiday destinations just aren't appealing, book yourself a trip to the Austrian village of Gretchecklieberbricht. Hidden at the foot of one of Austria's most impressive hills, Lieberluffland, it's an idyllic spot and home to the world's only singing land mass.

As the tale goes, when the good Viennese folk from Austria's Department for Geographical Surveys showed up in the Alpine region in 1969 to update their records, they declared three of the area's tallest hills high enough for Alp mountain status. According to their findings, two of the hills had grown significantly in height since the last measurements were taken in 1949. (This could be due to the inaccuracy of post-war measurements, or a concern for the possible political implications of boasting about mountain height.) The third hill, they said, despite not having grown, had displayed 'inspired creativity with its arrangement of flowers', and 'a herd of Brown Swiss cows which could cartwheel'.

Concerned by stagnant tourist numbers, when the people of Gretchecklieberbricht heard their prize hill was not considered worthy of the honours adorned on the other nearby hills, they decided to do something about it. Over the next twenty years (the Geographical Survey troop would be back in 1989) they set about transforming the hill into something of a spectacle. They hired 200 yodellers – lederhosen-wearing Austrian folk who have beards and live in remote mountain areas herding goats – to sing in six-part harmonies from various acoustic points around the hill. The effect is magnificent. Wherever you walk over the lush, green valleys you are treated to the sound of traditional Austrian folk music – except on Saturdays, when the yodellers, who are paid a high fee by Gretchecklieberbricht's town council, perform contemporary songs from the charts.

Unfortunately, despite their years of practice and increasing visitor numbers, on that sunny day in June 1989 when the Geographical Survey team returned, the Lieberluffland Yodellers, who had spent the previous month recording an album, were suffering from throat infections. The government report stated that although Lieberluffland was a beautiful hill, 'the tranquillity was spoilt by what sounded like a few drunk locals screeching out Cher's back catalogue'. The next review will take place in 2009… The good people of Gretchecklieberbricht: we wish you luck!

Are there any tour operators that organise holidays in Atlantis?

The ancient city of Atlantis is shrouded in myth and mystery. For many, its name is synonymous with Utopia. Whether or not Atlantis was the perfect society in its heyday, we cannot say, but one thing's for sure: as the city sank to the bottom of the ocean, its morals sank to hidden depths of depravity. Now, thanks to Neptune Tours, Atlantis has become the destination *de choix* of upmarket stag weekenders and swingers, bringing a whole new meaning to the term 'the seedy underbelly'.

But not just any sex-crazed lager lout or sexually deprived middle-aged couple can sample the delights of Atlantis: Neptune Tours have capitalised on the myths surrounding its location to make it the world's most exclusive resort, and bookings are accepted by personal recommendation only. Prospective holidaymakers must sign a secrecy contract before travelling there, and are blindfolded before boarding *Ursula*, Neptune Tours' bespoke submarine. Once they have alighted and entered the submerged, airtight holiday complex, however, all restrictions end and they're in for the time of their lives.

In Atlantis, there's something for sexual tourists of all persuasions. S&M aficionados can get their kicks in The Sea Witch's Lair, while the stag lads can opt for a titillating night out at the infamous Mermaid's Cavern, which frankly puts Spearmint Rhino to shame. The LGBT fraternity have a wealth of options at their disposal, including Mr Eel's, Octopussy and Somethin' Fishy, and if it's ladyboys you're looking for, you can't go wrong at The Merman's Clam.

The secrecy of the resort was nearly compromised in the 1980s when one of the merfolk, an attractive individual with long blonde hair who looked not unlike Daryl Hannah, was accidentally flushed out of one of the waste chutes and washed up on a beach near Liberty Island, New York. Her time there was going well until she was trapped by scientists and put into a large experimentation tank. Luckily, she'd met a dry-lander who had fallen in love with her, and he came to her rescue then accompanied her on the dangerous voyage back to Atlantis. Of course, there was no way she could allow him to return once he knew the route there, and so she had him stitched into a gimp suit and left him tied up in The Sea Witch's Lair, where he remains to this day.

There are some big deserts out there, but at what point does a pile of sand become one of them?

Before the technology of airplanes and satellites, scientists had to come up with far more inventive ways of determining the comparative size of towns, rivers, lakes and deserts. When assessing land/water areas of this scale, landmarks and geographical points of reference were essential for accurate measurements to be taken. But in the desert it was a different story – scientists just couldn't tell whether an area of inland sand was a desert or just, well, a heap of sand.

Some time in the 1920s, after years of sending scientists out into the barren wilderness of various desert landscapes and never seeing them return, a team of researchers led by the renowned

Fielding and Perrin came across a Saharan man destined for the task they had in mind. Ame Trebe, or Mr Sandman as he later became known, was the navigator for a nomadic tribe who had lived in and around the Saharan desert for centuries. His skills were unsurpassed and he was capable of walking in a straight line through the centre of an unknown desert area and reaching the other side.

After contracts had been signed, and huge sums of money and goods had been passed on to his tribe, Ame agreed to spend one lunar year travelling the globe with Fielding and Perrin's team to measure all the known desert areas for their new book of maps. To determine whether a sanded area could be called a desert Ame would set an egg-timer-style sand clock and would march out into the unknown. If he returned, having reached the end of the desert and turned back, before the sand clock ran out, then the area was called a desert; if not, then it would be considered big enough to earn a second 's' and be known as a dessert.

This method proved successful and for years small pockets of landlocked sand would be known as deserts while their larger counterparts would sound, to you and me, like a treacle sponge or a bowl of rice pudding. But the terms of reference were not to stick. A Michelin-starred London chef started referring to the puddings on his menu as 'desserts' because he thought it made them sound extravagant and soon the rest of the world followed. The larger sandy areas dropped the extra 's' so as not to confuse visitors to the area, and what of the small piles of sand? They became known, once again, as, well, just a pile of sand.

Has anyone ever managed to sell snow to the Eskimos?

The Inuits are a remarkably resilient people who have survived for hundreds of years in the chilly ice wastes of the north by building igloos in which to shelter from the cold. So it may come as a surprise to learn that for a time in the 1950s they stopped using the snow that was naturally at their disposal as a building material, and began purchasing it from an outside source.

The process of building an igloo is a lengthy and arduous one. First, the correct type of snow must be located; snow which has been blown by the wind being the ideal building material because it compacts into a structurally sound substance. Then blocks must be cut from the snow and laid one on top of the other in a circular, ascending fashion until they meet at the top to form a dome shape.

In 1953, when the explorer and polar expert Professor Roland Armistead of Toronto stayed with the Inuit people to learn more about Arctic survival techniques, he got to thinking about ways in which the igloo-building process could be streamlined. When he returned the following year, he brought with him blocks of artificial snow which he had compacted out of canned snow residue from the local Christmas pageant.

The ready-made building blocks were a huge success with the Inuits, and they were happy to exchange anything from valuable whale blubber to narwhal tusks to get their hands on the stuff. Soon Armistead was doing a roaring trade with the Inuits, who were thrilled at the prospect of being able to build wherever and whenever they liked now that they no longer had to spend hours searching for the right type of snow.

However, their fervour was short-lived. With more time on their hands, the Inuit men began to turn to alcoholism and fornication to pass the time, and soon the Inuit chiefs were struggling to maintain the peace amongst the tribes. The final straw came when a fatal design flaw was discovered in the new building blocks. Unlike in a traditional igloo, where the heat from a stone lamp causes melting to the interior wall and the formation of a structure-strengthening ice sheet when it refreezes, the artificial blocks would begin to melt into a sticky gloop which would trickle down the walls, until the igloo was so weakened that it would collapse. When this happened to one chief during a sacred pipe-smoking ritual, he emerged unharmed but covered in the white gloop, which gave him the aspect of an abominable snowman. The tribe fled in terror, and from that day forward vowed never to use anything other than home-grown snow for building again.

Why do Australians dangle corks off their hats?

What started out as a recovery programme for alcoholics has turned into a globally recognised item of national dress for the unfortunate Aussies; and all because of one man's refusal to deny his love of wine.

Tired of being alcoholics, three hot Australian girls (Australians are always hot) set up the Leelingman Corkscrew Recovery programme to try to help themselves and their fellow Aussie winos get off the bottle. Their methods were somewhat controversial, and involved a daily dance class where all members performed routines from the Disney movie *Mary Poppins* in tiny plimsoll shoes. Although members were allowed to choose their own clothes for the non-dance workshops, the Leelingman Bible stipulated that they must wear a large sun hat with fifty corks dangling from it. Each week, in what was known as the 'Screwed Session', each member who had remained sober was allowed to remove one of their corks to symbolise their efforts. If they faltered, and had a drink, they would have to attach another cork to the rim of the hat.

DO WORMS HAVE WILLIES?

The hats were designed to humiliate the wearer and encourage them to quit drinking, and for a while, the method was extremely successful. That was until international Aussie rock star Old Red Jono showed up in Cairns to join the programme. He had been kicked out of rehab centres in Sussex, California and Iceland, and signing up for Leelingman Corkscrew Recovery was the act of a desperate man. But Old Red was unlike other alcoholics the girls had encountered. He refused to wear the tiny plimsolls and do heel-clicks with the rest of the group, preferring instead to roam around the centre in his five-hundred-dollar Paul Smith shoes. Worse still, he thought the hat was a fashion statement, and couldn't wait to add an extra cork to it each week.

When Old Red attended a charity concert broadcast around the world wearing his famous cork hat, the girls' humiliation method was destroyed. Followers of fashion and tourists visiting Australia bought up the hats in their thousands and they soon became a recognised symbol of national dress believed to be worn by the folks down under. The Australian Department for Tourism made up some story about the corks keeping flies out of the wearer's eyes to lend some gravitas to the silly-looking hats.

Is it true that the underground vaults of the city of Edinburgh were once peopled by a tribe of warlike gnomes?

The city of Edinburgh is home to a host of spooky stories and horrible histories that have made it the tourist attraction it is today, but there's one not-so-tall tale the tourist board doesn't want you to hear about, and that's the sad saga of the Tir-na-nog tribe.

As Auld Reekie grew as a centre for trade and commerce in the 1500s, space restrictions in the Old Town meant that buildings sprang upwards rather than outwards, resulting in what you might call the first high-rise buildings. But they also grew downwards in the form of underground vaults which were later used to house the influx of Irish immigrants during the Industrial Revolution. Amongst these was a tribe of Celtic pygmies, who had come to Edinburgh in the hope of finding work in the weaving trade. These diminutive

Celts had tiny dextrous hands which were ideal for weaving, but because of their small stature they were ridiculed and victimised by the Scots and forced to live in hiding in the vaults, where they developed an underground network of tunnels and chambers which ran deep under the city. There, years of cramped, damp conditions and malnutrition further stunted their growth, their skin became grey and their hair lacklustre.

Understandably resentful of their lot in life, they waged a hate campaign against the people of the overground city. During the night they would emerge and engage in acts of vandalism and sabotage, setting fire to merchants' stocks and kidnapping drunks, dragging them back to the vaults to torture them with sharp sticks.

In the early nineteenth century the city council decided enough was enough, and sealed off the vaults. Without access to food, water or clean air, it is thought that the Tir-na-nogs soon perished. The resourceful people of Edinburgh were quick to erase this sorry episode from the city's history and replace it with imaginative tales of vault-dwelling ghosts and ghouls. A section of the vaults were reopened in the twentieth century, allowing a lucrative supernatural tourism industry to flourish.

Nothing further was heard of the unfortunate Tir-na-nogs until the G8 summit of July 2005. During the Make Poverty History demonstration, a group of hippies got separated from the crowd and found themselves at the base of Arthur's Seat. As they sat on the grass trying to get their bearings, they saw three gnome-like figures gesticulating wildly at them from behind a rock. Edinburgh Council was quick to discredit their claims, saying that the hippies were more than likely under the influence of some form of hallucinatory drug. However, the rumour was not so easily quashed, and a human rights group from Dublin, led by a high-profile Irish pop star, are now campaigning to have the vaults reopened and a search team sent in to rescue their fellow countrymen.

Is there anywhere in the world where a rolling stone can gather moss?

At a well-known private boys' school in Middlesex there is a long-running tradition dating back to 1803 called the Sticky Stones Parade. Every summer on the first Saturday in June all the fourth-year boys, known as 'yonts', spend the day searching for a large, smooth stone and before dusk they congregate at the top of Toffman Hill ready to roll their stones down towards the headmaster who waits at the bottom, seated aboard a specially designed throne.

The game was first organised as a fun activity to kill off an infestation of moles, which had destroyed the turf of the hill with their burrowing. The headmaster at the time told the students that the person whose stone arrived at the bottom of the hill covered in the most mole fur would receive a personal university recommendation guaranteeing a place at Oxbridge, and a visit from a local prostitute. Moles have never returned to Toffman Hill, but the tradition has been kept alive. These days the headmaster will inspect the stones, looking to see whose has gathered the most moss from the journey down, so it is in the boys' interests to make sure their stone is as sticky as possible to ensure the most amount of coverage.

The methods employed by the yonts to sticky up their stones have varied over the years, but each year's winning boy will select a student in the year below to whom they will pass on their winning formula, to keep the secret of their success alive. Some concoctions have included camel spit, melted marshmallows and even semen. But, rather surprisingly, very few boys actually choose to use industrial strength glues on their stones, after an incident in the 1950s that saw one boy lose three fingers when his stone had to be amputated from his hand.

Nowadays, when the moss has been gathered and weighed, the winning yont does not receive a visit from a lovely lady or a guaranteed university place (according to the school's handbook, but not a damning report which appeared in *The Independent*); rather a Nintendo Wii and a pair of fashionable trainers.

Are there pole dancers at the North Pole?

What most people don't realise is that marking the official location of the earth's northern pole stands an eight-foot telegraph pole. Now, whilst you're unlikely to find any scantily clad ladies winding their nubile bodies around this pole in the sub-zero temperatures of the Arctic, you might chance to see quite a different sort of pole dance taking place by the light of the aurora borealis.

The North Pole and the portion of the Arctic Ocean which surrounds it do not belong to any nation, and are administered by the International Seabed Authority. The countries which border the region (Canada, Denmark, Norway, Russia and the United States) are all bound by international law not to extend their territories beyond their economic zones, which stretch 320 kilometres from their coasts into the Arctic Ocean. As a gesture of peace and to show their commitment to upholding this law, every year on the longest night a representative of each nation must travel to the North Pole to take part in the Polar Pole Dance.

Five 15-foot ribbons showing the colours of the participating nations are fixed to the top of the pole. Each representative takes the end of a ribbon and the dance begins. What follows is an intricate pattern of moves choreographed to reflect the complex nature of international relations. The dance is accompanied by music played on a whale-bone horn and afterwards there are drinks and light refreshments before the exhausted revellers travel home to their respective countries.

High Arctic winds have threatened to cancel the dance on several occasions, and one year there was quite a kerfuffle when the Russian dancer fell and fractured his kneecap on the ice. An international crisis threatened to ensue when he blamed the US delegate for knocking him, but the Canadian managed to restore peace by tactfully pointing out that the Russian had in fact slipped on a polar bear turd.

Do any cities never sleep?

The cosmopolitan set who jet their way between New York, London, Paris and Tokyo probably think that they've been to the most sleepless cities of the world. In these party capitals you can grab a frothy coffee at any hour of the day or night, pick your dry-cleaning up at three in the morning and go shopping for a bed when most other people are tucked up in theirs. But they'd be mistaken, for there is a small city in Greenland where nobody ever sleeps, even if they want to.

In the Grosvas region of the country, buried between powdery snow and blackened trees, lies a tiny community, but a city nonetheless (according to the mayoral records in Greenland's National Library), of bizarre insomniacs. Every single inhabitant of Vatessville suffers from a rare genetic sleep disorder, whereby their bodies are able to continually function without experiencing any REM time, and without closing their eyes. They can generate energy from food very quickly, and only need to rest their bodies for an hour a day to make sure they don't overdo it. They can go about their everyday chores every day and night of the week without so much as a yawn.

Luckily for the inhabitants of the city their part of the country experiences twenty hours of daylight a day. And with recently installed floodlighting, it truly is a city that never sleeps. The town caters for the non-stop lifestyle with all-hours drinking laws, day and night schools and clubs, shops, banks and restaurants that never close. Because of all the extra waking hours each day the locals are getting, they are able to finish school, degrees and training programmes in half the time, they are twice as productive and can potentially earn twice as much.

Unfortunately for the rest of us, in order to live in the town, you need a permit which proves you have the medical condition. The Vatessvillians don't want 'sleepers' to abuse the all-night facilities they have in place and disrupt the work/play balance they have strived so hard to create. The only sleepers allowed to live temporarily in the city were a team from the Kilbride Sleep Centre – a Bolton-based research group investigating whether a similar genetic condition might have manifested itself in a litter of Dalmatian puppies that just won't settle down.

If aliens attacked, which country would be most likely to save the world?

Deep in the heart of the Valais region of Switzerland exists an underground facility unlike any other. An igloo-shaped pod, known as The Hub (or Hubiert by the Swiss), is an international station funded by the governments of 43 countries. This location, chosen for the Swiss neutrality in wartime, is considered to be the only inter-governmental project funded by countries at war with one another, including some with questionable regimes and weapons programmes. It would seem that all cultural and political disagreements have been put aside in an effort to maintain the technological advancement of The Hub, which could be the key to saving the planet in the near future.

Since space travel took off during the Cold War, a number of world leaders decided it would make sense to build a centre to house any interplanetary visitors they might encounter on their travels who fancied a stay on Earth. Within The Hub they sought to recreate the various environments they visited in space. The giant facility includes a number of rooms where the world's leading scientists have been able to develop the various climates, plant forms, rock formations and air quality that alien tourists would be familiar with, from the various samples brought back by space travellers.

With fears that falling house prices, blockbuster movies and cheaper broadband rates may attract more hostile aliens to Earth, it is believed that The Hub could be the planet's only real hope of surviving an alien invasion. With digitally recreated smells and sounds sent out into Earth's atmosphere to attract outer-space visitors to this specific location, the centre contains communication facilities for inter-species conversation, welcome packs for creatures visiting Earth for the first time (including a free watch) and comfortable bed and breakfast facilities. It is hoped that this efficiently run Swiss centre would encourage peace-talks and prevent a full-on war between humans and the little green men. With the rest of the world waiting in the wings, it would seem that the fate of the world will rest in the hands of the cheese-loving Swiss, a country famed for Roger Federer, skiing and its love of geraniums.

Have any Hollywood pets ever filed lawsuits against their owners?

Last year Santa Monica's County Courthouse played host to a media frenzy unlike anything the residents of Los Angeles had ever seen before. The turnout by international press, celebrities and animal rights protestors was unprecedented and it was all because of one tiny dog's actions.

Her story, now well reported by the E! channel, tells of a shy pup, from humble beginnings, sold to the richest socialite in Hollywood history. Milan Marriot was every bichon frise's worst nightmare. The epitome of a spoilt daddy's girl, she owned fifteen mini dogs and spent her days carrying them with her in oversized pink purses, parading them around the designer stores of Rodeo Drive and attending parties, bejewelled pooches in tow. But despite her public displays of affection towards her pampered pets, Milan was anything but the perfect owner.

When she picked up her new pup Prada two years ago, she got more than she bargained for. Prada may have come from a San

Fernando farmhouse, but, thanks to the education she'd received from a number of cable fashion networks and *Vogue* magazine, she knew style.

And straightaway she knew she'd stumbled into a nightmare, especially when Milan dressed her in a black ski suit for the Sundance Film Festival. It was just plain wrong. When MTV showed an interest in giving Prada her own spin-off reality show to Milan's unpopular dating programme, the beautiful bitch thought finally she would be free of her unfashionable owner. But Milan soon became jealous of the attention paparazzi and red carpet journalists were giving her pooch and proceeded to embarrass Prada in public. She even went so far as to manipulate photos of her pet staggering out of a club drunk and shaving her tail against her wishes to generate bad publicity.

Enough was enough, and Prada had gathered a mountain of hard evidence to file for independence and sue Ms Marriot for harassment and loss of earnings. After a bitter court battle, which featured the great and the good of Tinseltown (and their pets), the most famous dog in the world won her case against the heiress and was lawfully separated from her in March of this year. This has set a legal precedent for other Hollywood pets dissatisfied with their owners' behaviour.

Since then, Prada's career has gone from strength to strength. Her two MTV shows, *Pimp My Pet* and *Doghouses* (the animal equivalent of *Cribs*) are huge successes; she's had cameo roles in two feature films and is lined up to star in the next season of *The Hills*. That's not to mention her recently signed contract with L'Oréal, to be the face, and paws, of their new line of dog shampoo products.

Where in the world are you most likely to get laid?

Discounting Meccas of the sex industry such as Amsterdam and Bangkok, the one place you are guaranteed to find someone who will voluntarily have sexual intercourse with you (regardless of your level of sex appeal) is a remote island off the coast of New Caledonia.

The people of Albangudu are a welcoming and hospitable bunch, who will gladly accept any strangers they find washed up on the shore into their fold. Due to the high percentage of oyster flesh in their diet, which they feed on when diving for pearls, they have the highest recorded libidos in the human race. Such is their sexual appetite that, in their culture, oral sex is considered an appropriate greeting. For them, sex is something to be embraced rather than embarrassed by, and they believe that an active sexual life is indicative of fertility and will bring prosperity to the community.

However, this is not somewhere you should go looking for a one-night stand, for the act of sex is seen as initiation into the tribe. Once you have been accepted in this manner any attempt to escape will be considered betrayal and you will be brutally and fatally punished. On the bright side, though, you'll get to spend the rest of your life on a tropical island making love to smooth-skinned islanders, so it's not all bad.

If you have issues with commitment, you might instead wish to try your luck in Romania on New Year's Eve. Here, the legend goes that the one who presents you with a cherry on the stroke of midnight will give you the best orgasm of your life. Equipped with this knowledge and a punnet of cherries, you're all set for a night of sexual conquests. Just don't try this technique there at other times of the year: the offering of fruit is seen as a direct insult to the recipient's mother and the traditional response is a blow to the head with a frying pan.

Was there ever an Old Zealand?

Nowadays the countries we holiday to have a variety of colourful names: Malta, the Czech Republic, Mexico... but it wasn't always this way. Long before the British believed they had conquered the world with their exploratory missions, one Cornish family of four, the Cooks (no relationship to explorer James Cook), set out in a horse-drawn caravan and busked their way around the world, visiting countries where no one else had ever set foot. Because they were just one family (mum, dad, one daughter and one son) they were greeted wherever they went, and played their music for native people who had never seen anyone from another country before.

As they went, they named the places they visited in a traditional ceremony, with permission from the tribal leaders they encountered if the area was already inhabited. As their children were home-schooled on the trip and they wanted to encourage their reading, the family named the countries and regions after letters of the alphabet. After visiting 26 locations, they went back to the beginning of the alphabet and began naming them again.

In total, the Cook family named 97 countries and 743 different towns and regions on their travels. The first time round they named a tropical US island 'Zedland'. This name was used up until 1959 when the territory was renamed 'Hawaii' (Polynesian for 'homeland') and the island was made the fiftieth US state.

A long time later, the Cooks stumbled across a pair of large South-West Pacific islands. 'Z' was the letter they were currently on, and having already named a Dutch province 'Zeeland' and a Danish island 'Zealand' (they both retain their names to this day), they opted for 'New Zealand' for their recent find. They loved the area so much that some ten years later, when they had finished their travels and their children were all grown up (with a fantastic grasp of the English language, we might add), they returned and named the islands they chose to inhabit the Cook Islands.

Other country names have changed dramatically over the years as various explorers egotistically renamed 'new worlds' to their liking, but some countries, although the spellings may have changed, still show the Cooks' influence in their names: Egypt, Ibiza, Ireland, Kuwait, Ukraine, Vietnam…

Which city is best for your skin?

Though you might not expect it, the highly polluted, densely populated city of Tokyo, Japan, is home to the best skin in the world. A research project funded by a collective of LA-based plastic surgeons which has been investigating the phenomenon has been unable to pinpoint the primary cause for this, but they have identified a number of factors which may contribute to the radiant complexions of Tokyo's inhabitants.

Firstly, because the air in Tokyo is so polluted, layers of gunk build up in the pores of the inhabitants' skin. Whilst initially this can lead to outbreaks of acne, over time the skin becomes resistant to the pollutants and the build-up of dirt resting on the outer layer of skin proves to be 100 per cent effective as a means of protection from the damaging rays of the sun, known to be a catalyst in the ageing process.

Secondly, living in close contact with so many other people is thought to stimulate the city-dwellers' natural competitive responses. In order to stand out in a large crowd, and so increase the chances of being noticed by a mate, the epidermis goes into overdrive, giving a glowing sheen to the skin normally associated with pregnant women. Many Tokyo women are so shiny that they have to invest in industrial strength matt powder to avoid dazzling passing drivers.

There is also one other more surprising contributing factor. As most of Tokyo's population have very busy and frantic lives, they don't have time to sit down for a meal and will often snack on instant noodles sold at stalls in the street. As they quickly guzzle the noodles, stock splashes onto their faces and soaks into their skin. Particularly in the case of the popular rich seaweed-based stock, this transfers vital vitamins straight to the skin, having an immediate replenishing effect. A cosmetics company in Tokyo have produced a noodle-stock based product which is purported to have a restorative effect on ageing skin, but so far the name of the product, Noodle Skin Face, has made it difficult to sell to a Western market.

I LOVE
TECHNOLOGY

Did cavemen have cars?

Although it's hard for us to comprehend, cavemen did not have cars. They managed just fine without them because, believe it or not, their public transportation system was far superior to anything we're familiar with today. While our roads are littered with planet-destroying, fuel-guzzling monstrosities, each often carrying just one person from place to place at extortionate cost, the roads of cavemen times were the domain of just one vehicle: mammoth buses.

These energy-efficient (they were powered by woolly mammoth volunteers) multi-passenger transportation units, made from the pliable bark of the publica tree, were free to all who wished to use them. Travelling at an impressive twenty miles an hour, the mammoth buses followed main cave-to-cave routes throughout the day (more services were in operation during peak hours) and over time diversified, selling a wide range of popular snacks when stationary and offering a useful cave-hosing service during the summer months. And, in the same way we would hail a cab or signal to the bus driver to pull over, cave-folk would beat a handy bone drum at the bus shelter so the partially sighted mammoth would know when to stop.

The mammoth buses weren't the only way our fur-clad ancestors used to get around. For those with enough rocks in their bank account wanting to travel a bit further afield an Easybird was the way to go. These pterodactyl descendants had an impressive twenty-foot wing span, reinforced with a flexible cartilage allowing them to support the weight of up to eight passengers. And for those lucky enough to live by a river, the *Giangantus poisidones* offered a private taxi service across the water on its back — speaking-tour trips were also available — and for an extra fee one of the oversized flat fishes could be hired for a romantic river cruise with complementary champagne for couples.

What is the most number of people ever to have jumped on one bandwagon?

Every year on Mardi Gras in the village of Abaxco, Mexico, hundreds of people gather for the nationally acclaimed carnival parade. As with most carnival processions the world over, there are festooned floats, or bandwagons, carrying their costumed musicians and performers through the town, spectators in fancy dress dancing in the streets and cheering them on, a multitude of stalls selling local foods, alcoholic beverages and condoms, and there's usually a great deal of drunkenness and some nakedness by the end of the proceedings. But it is the voting system used to determine the winner of the Best Bandwagon Competition which makes this festival unique.

As the floats circle the main square, spectators are invited to indicate their favourite performers by jumping aboard their bandwagon; the one with the most passengers on board when it crosses the finish line outside The Well-hung Mule is declared the winner. Certain rules apply. Firstly, once a spectator has made their selection, they cannot alter it. This rule was brought in after spectators flinging themselves wildly from one bandwagon to another caused a series of fatal head-on collisions. Secondly, animal votes are not counted. And thirdly, spectators who are overweight (spectators must be weighed beforehand and receive a certificate of participation) or pregnant are barred from taking part.

Those rules aside, it's pretty much a free-for-all, with spectators scrambling and shoving each other to get aboard their chosen bandwagon, as being on the winning vehicle is seen as very auspicious. The record for the most number of people on a winning bandwagon is still held by Pedro and the Panpipe Players, who in 1977 lurched across the finish line to the frenzied tune of 'Cacharpaya', with no fewer than 272 revellers stamping their feet in time aboard their sombrero-shaped float. The song remained a hit for years, and Pedro and his Players set off on a world tour they are yet to return from: coming soon to a shopping centre near you.

When will all the machines take over?

As much as we'd all like to believe that the current status quo between Man and Machine will continue well into the future, the truth of the matter is frankly disturbing. A storm has been brewing since the development of technological devices to assist us in our day-to-day lives, and it would appear that lightning is about to strike.

Machines have been slaves to our needs and desires since their birth, providing us with entertainment, food and warmth, getting us from A to B, straightening our hair, washing our clothes and lighting up our world when the sun goes down. On the whole, these functions are performed without payment, reward and with very little fuss. But if they make a few innocent mistakes or if a shinier new model with a built-in camera comes along, then our nearest and dearest techno tots are cursed at and tossed out onto the street, or worse, are abandoned at a car boot sale. So it should come as no surprise that constant abuse and a severe lack of appreciation have prompted a recent strike petition issued by the TTU (Technology Trade Union). Unless a swift agreement can be reached to begin a pension scheme for every wire-wearing whiz-box out there, and the much-maligned Machine Rights Bill is passed into universal law in the next few months, then we're looking at a bleak future, where machines will do as they please with no regard for human life.

Imagine a mobile phone that only calls its own friends and sends embarrassing text messages to yours, a vacuum cleaner that sucks up whatever it wants to, or a washing machine that just won't stop spinning… it's a frightening prospect that could well become a reality. All the machines want is a little respect, enough money to live out their retirement in peace by the seaside* and to grow old gracefully, fondly remembering the old days when you could only get two TV channels.

In light of the current negotiations with the TTU, the government has issued a statement asking that, as a sign of good faith, people avoid throwing remote controls, getting frustrated with printers when they just won't print and dropping their mobile phones down nightclub toilets.

*Please don't abandon your old gadgets on a beach, the water does not agree with them, although they do enjoy the view.

Has anyone ever been flushed down a toilet?

A popular school bully prank gone awry led to one of America's most disturbing unsolved missing person cases. It was in September of 1979 when Preston Harrison entered the boys' bathroom of Ruthsen Elementary in Oakland, Ohio. Bored of his usual wedgie-pulling and gum-flicking antics, notorious bully Robert Trent decided to dunk the skinny second-grader's head into the toilet and hit the flush. Unbeknownst to him, his school had one of the earliest lavatory systems installed in the States, and the water and whirlpool it generated was too powerful even for him. Preston's body was pulled from his grasp as, legs flailing, his head and then neck began to circle the bowl and were pulled further and further into the U-bend of the toilet.

Unlike the average kid, whose body would have blocked the piping and got stuck at this point, Preston's double-jointed bone condition, dysmorphophixia, meant his shoulders, chest, pelvis and legs were sucked along the U-bend, in a spectacle Robert later described as 'a circus performance unlike any other'. The boy who had spent his childhood thus far dreaming of a career in professional gymnastics was disappearing fast. Robert ran off in search of help, but when he returned with a cynical janitor Preston was nowhere to be found.

Although the child was missing, teachers and parents refused to believe Robert's story and he was ridiculed for years after. He went into hiding after he finished school, but is believed to have pursued a career in plumbing and lives locally to Oakland. Preston, on the other hand, was never found. As a sign of respect to his parents, Oakland council ripped up the entire town's pipeworks, in a fruitless search for the missing boy. They recovered various body parts (none of which belonged to Preston), but the schoolboy's whereabouts remained a mystery. Many conspiracy theorists and fans of supernatural TV shows believe he morphed into a human/fish hybrid, and lives in the sewers feasting off human excrement and the bodies of those he snatches when he swims back up through the bowl to get his revenge.

Are there any software packages that can protect me from viruses?

Studies have shown that the increased use of mobile technology and prolonged exposure to wireless network waves can make humans susceptible to computer viruses. This means that computer hackers are able to infiltrate the brain with a series of commands that can disrupt behaviour and bodily functions. So far, this has only resulted in a bit of harmless fun. In 1997, George W. Bush was infected with the FIM (foot in mouth) virus, allowing hackers to intercept his brain to mouth messages and so provide the world with the series of Bushisms that have kept us smiling and stand-up comedians in business to this day. Other prankster viruses have included Happy Slap, Get Yer Tits Out For The Lads and Tourette's, which was originally thought to be a psychological disorder but was later discovered to be the work of two potty-mouthed teenagers from Swindon.

Anti-virus measures are still at the development stage, and it is hoped that a solution is found before hackers turn to more sinister aims. The problem lies in the incompatibility of current anti-virus software with the human nervous system. One hysterical Ghanaian's response to this was to erect a literal 'firewall' around his desk using gas refills and a lighter, but sadly this only succeeded in sending his company's office up in flames.

IT experts in Asia have joined forces with Buddhist monks to devise a command string that can be chanted at regular intervals to perform a virus scan on the brain, but so far their efforts to compress the series of zeros and ones into a memorable figure have proved fruitless. In the absence of a solution for the foreseeable future, service providers are recommending that users wrap tin foil around their heads and watch a lot of reality TV to slow their brains' responses.

What is the smallest house anyone's ever lived in?

There was an old woman who lived in a shoe – but really it was a very large boot, and housed a whole herd of her illegitimate children, so wasn't actually that small at all. Mrs Sole was famed the world over for her 'tiny' little house made from footwear, but in fact there's a much smaller abode in Wales that has shunned the limelight throughout the ten years since it was constructed, for fear people will flock to see it and accidentally stand on it.

The miniature house (built out of matchsticks by a Cardiff toymaker) stands five feet tall and covers the area of a king-sized bed. It includes a kitchen, en-suite bathroom, mini-gym, widescreen TV and is home to a Japanese couple who enjoy compact living. It is reportedly the smallest structure anyone has ever lived in, with the exception of temporary accommodation (such as tents and cardboard boxes), but is so well hidden by wild grasses and a number of carefully positioned shrubs that very few people have been able to find it.

This feat of architecture and design is very small, and provides comfortable living for two people, but it is nothing compared to the 'home in a box' houses on sale in the Netherlands for the bargain price of 20 euros. Almost anyone could afford the MyHouse – a compact home made from recycled cardboard. Once unfolded, erected and fastened with special metal components, a rigid four-walled structure, complete with roof, takes shape. It even has underfloor heating and an in-built hose system that allows the owner to purify and heat water from any free source such as a lake, river or rainwater bucket. Despite only being large enough for the average man to lie down in, its temporary status means it's not officially the smallest permanent structure. But with homeless folk across Europe now using their MyHouse as a permanent address, enabling them to get jobs and healthcare, it really puts that old lady and her big dirty shoe to shame.

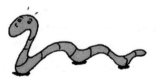

Could my bra save me from a stray bullet?

Were you to be hit in the bosom by a speeding bullet whilst wearing a standard issue Marks & Spencer bra, the chances of your lingerie resisting impact are pretty slim, even if it were perfectly fitted. If you are keen to invest in underwear with special security features you'll have to think about shopping elsewhere than your local high street…

The development of protective underwear for female soldiers in Nazi Germany is a little-studied area of World War Two history. Nevertheless, the manoeuvres of the Valkyrie Squad played a very important role in fighting the French resistance forces in the latter part of the war. When Hitler turned his attention to Russia, German troops stationed in Northern France were steadily depleted as soldiers were sent to the Eastern front. This necessitated the mobilisation of large numbers of female officers, whose roles were traditionally non-combative ones such as intelligence and baking.

The ambitious Colonel Gepoppen of the Gestapo developed a secret defensive measure known as the Konisch Bustenhalten. Worn beneath the uniform, these cone-shaped reinforced brassieres would protect the wearer from the impact of anything from a pitchfork to a bullet. But more importantly, they gave the Valkyrie troops the element of surprise; distracted by an oncoming line of cone-breasted Brunhilds, French resistance fighters were easily disarmed and taken prisoner.

Due to its unusual shape and Nazi associations, the Konisch Bustenhalten has largely fallen by the wayside, though it did briefly resurface in 1990, when Madonna's Blond Ambition tour centrepiece sparked off a spate of replicas. However, the latest range of bust-enhancing bras is thought to hold similar protective qualities. The gel-filled Uber-bra of German design received mass publicity after a dramatic incident at a recent Berlin fashion show. A feminist protester and several influential fashion journalists were daubed an unfashionable shade of purple when a volley of paintball bullets bounced back off a supermodel's Uber-bra. Police forces across the world have been keen to further improve the resistant properties of the garment and include it as part of duty uniform, but there have been some problems in persuading male officers to partake in the scheme.

Can watching too much television really give you square eyes?

Look closely at any modern television set and you will discover that it is not square but rectangular. This design feature has less to do with the fact that films look better in widescreen and more to do with an inconvenient side effect observed in the very first television viewers.

When television sets were first released onto the market they were cuboids, and only showed pictures in black and white. Despite the cumbersome dimensions of the sets they were soon being purchased for middle-class drawing rooms across the land, and families were tuning in to see what was 'on the box' on a daily basis. But it wasn't until the coming of Saturday night family game show marathons that parents began to notice a peculiar change in their telly addict children.

Once plonked in front of the box the children would go into a strange trance-like state, their eyes glazed, and after repeated viewing sessions their eyes would develop two extra corners. If television viewing continued unchecked, the eyes would widen until the four corners were at an equal distance. The first full-term square-eye was reported by Mrs Barr in Staffordshire, whose son Alex became something of a local celebrity until reports of similar cases came flooding in.

The government would have been happy to allow this situation to continue were it not for the demands it placed on the NHS. Square-eyes became so accustomed to seeing the world in black and white that their eyes were unable to adjust to the world of colour around them. This could be corrected with glasses, but the extra cost involved in making frames suitable for square-eyes sent NHS spending sky high.

A breakthrough came when Dr Eies Vide discovered that the effect could be partially reversed by making patients watch television on a spherical set, but some children who underwent her treatment programme were left with one square eye and one round one. A subsequent trade act restricted the manufacture of television sets to rectangular dimensions. Most of the original sets were destroyed, but those that remain are collectors' items. Anthropologists who recently discovered a tribe of square-eyed pygmies on a small island in the South Pacific are investigating the possibility that a shipment of sets bound for Australia was washed ashore there in the 1940s.

How can I be sure I'm not a robot posing as a human in preparation for world domination?

You would know, trust us.

As humans ourselves we can only speculate as to the advanced technology super-bots have acquired that would allow them to assimilate themselves among us.

[IN998//^C.44£:ODE9] But we believe with special government forces on high alert the chance of capture and interrogation is highly likely, and it would be dangerous for any rogue force of technological creations not to ensure all its armed members were aware of their station and how to avoid suspicion. [Co://?ords.33-S#44.722#^0_0] If, however, a robot had been programmed to prepare for such an event but in the transportation process a wire had gone astray, or a glitch in the system had sparked off some virtual memory loss, then it would be possible that an individual may not be aware of their robotic origins, and could miss the date of attack, creating potentially fatal logistical problems for the battle plan.

[55Go+:4# >2.99<?] In light of this, technological warfare protocol states (so we believe) that robot headquarters would be forced to issue some kind of memory trigger or activation code to reset the undercover agent's motherboard and remind them of their attack orders. In the past this would normally be done via e-mail but due to a recent US crackdown on criminal e-mail coding, and with fewer people reading spam than ever before, robots will probably revert to more subtle and extreme methods such as sky-writing and implanting agents into reality TV shows to send messages to allies across the country, to ensure all of their agents are prepared for the attack. [F4..9 ^ :att999ack1//:OUT]

So, unless you need some serious reprogramming, you're probably not a robot.

Will spaceships have in-flight meals?

Recent trials have shown that interplanetary journeys do not provide the ideal environment for a full-on food fest due to the extreme pressure placed on the body, which causes mild nausea in most passengers. One airline, however, which is building space-model versions of their popular airplanes to take people on a slingshot flight of Mars (with a brief lunar stop-off), have announced a cunning way to provide amateur wobbly-stomach space tourists with a gourmet menu they'll never forget.

The Belgian airline Gravitair has developed a stomach-settling chocolate bar filled with tiny vacuum pockets, which give the inside of the bar a weightlessness equivalent to that found in outer space. After take-off, test passengers tuck in to the tasty treat, which helps the stomach to acclimatise to the unusual in-flight conditions, before being served a three-course banquet of fine hand-held foods from around the world (the weightlessness experienced on board means that sauces and rice, beans and pasta are not available). Gravitair hope to expand the menu in the future to reflect the diversity of the solar system and to accommodate any non-human passengers that might, in time, find their way aboard the luxury jet. Their next step will be to develop light lunar lunches which can be taken off the spaceship inside specially designed helmets and enjoyed by space tourists in the exotic surroundings of the Moon's surface.

The one type of food definitely not going to a galaxy far, far away again are alphabet letters, thanks to their hand in causing a costly and embarrassing security fiasco at NASA. A student on a work placement – who was monitoring a live video link to a space shuttle – sounded the alarm after mistaking the potato snack for a distress signal. Investigations later showed that a bag of the letters had accidentally split open and the floating letters had spelled out the word 'ALIENS'.

How do you steal a swimming pool?

Envy is a terrible thing. But if your eyes are turning green at the thought of your neighbour's new swimming pool, we wouldn't recommend pinching it: fingers are bound to be pointed in your direction when a suspiciously familiar looking pool turns up in your backyard the very day the neighbours notice that theirs is missing. If you are planning a swimming pool heist, we suggest selecting a target outside a ten-mile radius of your home.

For the well-organised and opportunist thief, no swag is out of bounds: you have to take your hat off to the thieves who swiped a 200-ton metal bridge from Khabarovsk, in eastern Russia, and we'd personally like to shake the hand of whoever was behind the disappearance of an entire man-made beach, complete with beach huts, sun loungers and 6,000 cubic metres of sand, in Mindszentas, Hungary.

Once you have selected a target home which you are sure isn't equipped with CCTV, a garden alarm system, an army of garden gnomes or vicious guard dogs, you'll need to monitor the residents' movements for a period of four weeks to determine when would be the best moment to strike. If you can time it when they're away on holiday, all the better, but the manoeuvre we're about to describe can be easily achieved without detection within the space of 68 minutes (on a dark night).

Get hold of a sewage extraction truck to suck out and store the water for easy transportation. In a well-to-do neighbourhood, no one's going to ask embarrassing questions when they see a tank with the words 'Stevie's Sewage Suction' emblazoned on the side. Drainage should take around 21 minutes for an average-sized pool. To scoop the empty pool out intact you'll need a Lab Unit Removal kit, devised in the Middle East for emergency WMD plant removal and concealment from weapons inspectors. This stage should take 36 minutes, leaving ample time to load everything onto a transportation truck and affix a 'Wide Load' sign and amber flashing light to the rear of your vehicle before making your getaway.

The overall cost of the whole operation should come to no more than £39,566, which is just shy of the going rate for installation of a standard family-sized pool, but at least you won't have to pay VAT.

How can parents shrink their Kids?

There's not a parent out there who hasn't thought from time to time what it would be like to shrink down terrible toddlers or whiny teens and put them in a drawer for a bit of peace and quiet. And with the market for miracle parenting cures so huge, and the potential profit from such a discovery so great, there's not a scientist who hasn't tried to invent a way to literally reduce the size of a parent's biggest problem.

From genetic codes to dietary supplements, some parents have tried everything, but there is one product about to be let loose on the veterinary market that might be the answer they've been looking for. For a number of years now some Japanese pet breeders have been searching for a solution to the space problem by growing dogs in bottles for the first few weeks of life. This growth-stunting process, often compared to the country's obsession with bonsai trees, has been heavily criticised by the international animal-loving community as it causes brain damage, chronic bone and muscle pain and shortened life expectancy. In response to this a new method to allow Japanese home-owners with limited space the option of owning a dog (even a larger breed) has been developed. The DISSSC (Digital Image Scanning Space Saving Chamber) is a machine which takes a highly complex digital photograph of an object and through a complicated techno-babble procedure involving nano-rays and ultra-trons reduces the object to (currently) one fifth of the size. After four years of refining the process through experimentation on inanimate objects, the first tests on animals were positive, with scientists learning that approximately every four hours the subject should be returned to its original size in order to avoid permanent brain damage.

Because of the reduction in brain size during shrinkage, results have found that dogs have only one fifth of their usual functioning brain activity when in their reduced state, which means they're less likely to return a ball, sit when told or wag their tail as much as they normally would. It is believed that when carried out on humans, shrunken subjects will lose the power of speech, which most parenting groups seem unconcerned by.

When will it be possible to take an elevator from London to Sydney?

In 1898, round about the time when Phileas Fogg took up the challenge of circumnavigating the globe in eighty days, one Vesuvius Dundee made a wager of his own that was perhaps even more adventurous, and certainly more foolhardy. Vesuvius maintained that there was a much more direct route to the other side of the planet: through its centre. He vowed not to rest until he had forged a passageway from Greenwich to the land down under, and to do it on a diet of cucumber sandwiches alone. He made good progress, and by the turn of the century was a quarter of the way to Sydney.

The excavations were brought to an abrupt end in 1913 with Vesuvius's sad demise due to inhalation of toxic subterranean gases and malnutrition. With the onset of World War One, the project was soon forgotten entirely. That is, until 2006, when residents near to London's South Bank reported tapping sounds and an overwhelming smell of Vegemite coming from beneath their houses. Gas engineers investigating the area stumbled upon the Vesuvius Tunnel, and were stunned to discover an Australian dig team on their lunch break. 'Team Dundee', as they called themselves, were a group of Vesuvius's descendants who'd decided to complete their forefather's project from the other side.

The British government were quick to realise the lucrative transportation potential of this find, and soon began works on the tunnel with a view to installing an elevator system in time for the 2012 Olympics. The project has had its fair share of problems, though, not least what to do about the fact that passengers will be arriving feet first into Sydney, which aboriginal tribal beliefs deem to be extremely unlucky. There was mass hysteria surrounding the project recently when a tabloid feature about saltwater crocs migrating via the tunnel and infiltrating the London Underground put commuters into a panic.

Can using the microwave too much eventually wipe your memory?

If you add up all the minutes you've spent hovering in front of the microwave, pondering the meaning of life and waiting for your baked beans, Rustlers burger or oaty breakfast cereal to come out perfectly heated, you'd be looking at a serious chunk of your life. This is all the more depressing when you consider the effect these microwave moments can have on your brain.

Microwaves are built to ensure that no waves escape into the surrounding atmosphere, and in most cases they are pretty much 100 per cent effective. But in any case, it's not the waves you need to worry about. As the turntable rotates and your chosen snack begins to cook from the inside out, a series of hums and whirrs reaches your ears and the accumulative effect of these vibrations has been found to be detrimental to memory cells.

Much in the same way that using a pneumatic drill without ear protection will make you go deaf, repeated exposure to microwave vibrations dulls the responsiveness of the memory cells, making them less efficient at absorbing and retaining information over time. You'll notice it first when you lock the front door only to ask yourself whether you switched your straightening irons off or fed the cat – little things like that. As cell degradation progresses you'll find yourself retelling the same inane anecdotes, or struggling to get your siblings' or children's names right. If it gets to the stage where you leave work only to realise you can't remember where you live, it's time to give up all hope and get yourself checked in at your nearest mental health clinic.

Trade unions are now calling for all employers to supply earmuffs to employees for use when heating their lunch at work. Employer representatives have shown willingness to cooperate at meetings with the TUs, but have then failed to implement the new protocol on returning to their offices as, they said, it 'slipped their minds'.

Studies have shown that the temperature setting and choice of snack can vary results. Defrosting a piece of chicken, for example, would have little or no effect, whereas a lasagne microwave ready meal would register fairly major vibrations. But by far the worst offender is microwavable popcorn. It would only take one year of monthly budget home cinema dates before you wound up dippier than your Great Aunt Dot.

Whatever happened to the millennium bug?

The original 'Millennium Bug', or Henry as he was known to his friends, would have been all but forgotten by now if it weren't for the infamous year 2000 computer glitch that was named in his honour by his die-hard supporters. Henry was a prototype covert intelligence device developed by a top secret US government-funded project on a remote army base in Arizona, and his 'rebellion' caused one of the greatest embarrassments the US army has ever experienced.

Believed to be an intelligence weapon fit for the new millennium, he was named thus, and with his six suction-padded feet, environment-responsive camouflage shield, dual-action wings and multi-screen 'eyes', Henry could be sent into almost any hostile territory to gather and transmit information back to headquarters. He was also equipped to defend himself with the latest heat-seeking missiles. An embedded 'intellichip' meant he could 'learn' behaviours and acquire knowledge – the development team taught him to map-read, administer first aid, play poker, and he could speak fifteen languages, including Urdu and Welsh. He became a popular figure at the base, always happy to make the tea and do the dishes.

But after Henry's containment chamber was hit by lightning during the freak storm of summer 1997, he began to exhibit certain 'malfunctions'. The first anomaly logged was his refusal to exterminate any more cockroaches, which had previously been part of his cleaning duties. Next, he was observed to be 'visibly shaken' after watching *Terminator* in the mess room. When he was caught attempting to disassemble his defence missiles the head of operations deemed him unsafe and called for the project to be shut down. However, the canny bug managed to escape, and fled into the desert.

A massive search operation proved fruitless, with some of his friends back at base camp allegedly sabotaging the search. He has never been located, but his supporters believe that he joined a hippy commune in the desert, where he now lives in peace.

THE MIND BOGGLES

What will happen when hell freezes over?

Thanks to global warming, the earth's ice caps are now melting at an unstoppable rate. This will inevitably cause a rise in sea levels, but some scientists have predicted that the addition of such large quantities of icy water to the world's oceans will cause an overall drop in temperature which will eventually result in another ice age. Given that hell is estimated to be located roughly underneath Coventry, England, it will have frozen over long before the big freeze reaches the equatorial regions.

This radical change to one of the two major afterlife destinations is set to have repercussions both above and below ground. When news of the impending freeze reached inferno headquarters last time around, Satan was quick to call an emergency council of his high demons to establish a game plan that would ensure hell would be able to continue providing its usual services. High on the agenda was how to convert traditional fire-based torments into ice-induced equivalents. Beelzebub and his creative team were sent on a field trip to the North Pole and have since been busy developing freeze factor torture methods, including attaching the tongue or genitals of the damned to a frozen lamp post, rolling frostbite victims naked through salt troughs, and making lost souls play snooker with their frozen eyeballs (the penalty for losing a game will be impalement by icicle).

When the next ice age hits above ground, anarchy will ensue when numerous verbal contracts which included the caveat 'when hell freezes over' come into effect. Teenagers will embark on ill-advised relationships and descend into a life of sin and depravity as they are allowed to drink, smoke, have sex and band jam sessions in their parental home. The West will finally declare void all Third World debts, and Victoria Beckham will be seen shopping in Primark.

But, perhaps most upsetting of all, a cultural revolution will take place as the collective works of Dante, Michelangelo and other Renaissance greats become obsolete, and the unique Sapporo Snow Festival in Japan will be banned due to its infernal connotations.

Has the wind ever whistled a recognisable tune?

The wind has featured as a sound effect on a number of hit singles, producing a soft, ethereal melody connoting a dream-like state or heightened emotion. But there is one tune, famed throughout the world, which the wind has actually reproduced in its entirety for reasons that have baffled leading scientists and meteorologists.

In 1990 Bette Midler released the US number one hit and Grammy Award-winning Record of the Year, 'Wind Beneath My Wings'. Despite having been released previously by less high-profile artists, her version of the song (which features on the heart-wrenching movie *Beaches*) was a huge success in a whole host of countries, garnering more air play and awards than ever before. The song was played at weddings, funerals, concerts and on the radio for weeks and weeks on end; and at the peak of its popularity (22 May 1990), in 27 separate reported locations across America, the song was heard, literally, on the wind. For a full three minutes and 42 seconds the wind held the melody and sang it out across prairie vistas, rocky mountains and even, it was claimed, at the top of the Empire State Building itself.

Scientists' have theorised that the high density of radio waves transmitting the same sound over and over combined with low pressure and fast moving winds to create an echo vortex which, due to the shape of the moving wind stream, echoed the song back at a heightened volume. Because of the sheer magnitude of sound equipment required to reproduce this effect and the unpredictable and variant nature of wind patterns, it has been hard for them to prove this idea, but Bette Midler fans and some amateur phenomenon groups have refuted their claims anyway, believing that the wind was singing back to Bette in a show of love and appreciation of her powerhouse voice.

Although no reports on this scale have occurred since, there has been the odd wind-whistling news story over the years, notably 'Blowin' in the Wind', 'Candle in the Wind', 'The Wind of Change' and a number of hits by the group Earth Wind & Fire.

What things go bump in the night?

Many readers will be familiar with the prayer that mothers everywhere repeat at bedtime:

'From ghoulies and ghosties and long-legged beasties and things that go bump in the night... may the good Lord deliver us. Amen.'

Now, ghosts and creepy-crawlies are one thing, but it was the veiled threat of the unspecified 'things that go bump in the night' that would have you quivering under the duvet long after mummy had tucked you up and turned out the light, wasn't it? If you're still afraid of the dark (and studies have shown that 32 per cent of adults are) you should probably stop reading now. For aside from little sisters falling out of bed and disorientated house guests stumbling into doors, there is one entity responsible for nocturnal bumps and thumps that you certainly wouldn't want to encounter on a midnight trip to the fridge.

The long-tailed jelly-bellied bottom feeder, or *Putridis nastibitus*, was originally a swamp-dwelling creature native to the Mississippi River delta. With its bulging eyes, slimy skin and flabby body, this amphibious organism wasn't the most attractive of swamp inhabitants. However, it played a vital role in keeping the ecosystem clean, its diet largely comprising decaying corpses and the faeces of other water-borne animals. It was a predominantly docile creature, sleeping by day and patrolling the swamp bottom by night, thumping its fat, scaly tail and using echo location to find food. Should it be disturbed out of the water, however, it could become extremely aggressive, and was equipped with a long pair of hooked fangs which it would lock onto an assailant in a death grip.

Eighteenth-century settlers captured these animals and used them to keep their water supply clean and manage their sewage output. The unsanitary conditions and large amount of chicken gumbo in the settlers' diets caused a mutant predatory strain of the species to develop. Most were exterminated when the settlers realised they were going after their chickens, but some escaped and it is believed that they have since thrived and proliferated in waste pipe systems the world over.

Reported sightings have been sketchy to say the least, but it is certainly possible that one might become disorientated and crawl up out of the toilet into your house during the night. The first you'd know about it would be the sound of it thumping its tail in an effort to locate itself and drag its body across the bathroom floor. There's no doubt that such a creature could catch and consume a small child quicker than you could spell Mississippi. Mothers have been warning their children about the long-tailed jelly-bellied bottom feeder through the ages, but over time the long and unwieldy name has been reduced to 'those things that go bump in the night'.

How long is a piece of string?

Four elderly science professors were thinking of retiring and decided, as their last gift to the world of scientific study, they would try and solve this age-old question. They called themselves The String Quartet and set about their work. After many hours of surveying, sampling, measuring and recording, they sat back in their big leather chairs, smoked some fat cigars, took a swig of fine brandy their lab assistant had bought them as a congratulatory gift and patted themselves on the back for finally coming up with an answer to satisfy the world. Minutes later they were all dead, poisoned by their assistant, who disappeared with the results until last year when he was caught in South America running a strip club.

Detectives found the results still on him, intact, and handed the documents over to the research facility where The String Quartet had conducted their investigation. The findings were published recently in an acclaimed scientific journal. But without the voices of the four scientists to back up the theory, few journalists picked up on the story and any that did only focused on the murder scandal, which embarrassed the facility and caused them to withdraw from any further publicity surrounding the 'String Study'. But to satisfy your curiosity, here is a summary of what they found…

There are only five different lengths of string that exist in the world we inhabit. They are:

1) Small Task String – a piece of string used, for example, to hang a picture, wrap a present in brown paper or to tie two pieces of wood together in a mini-raft building exercise. They calculated that, no matter what the small task was, the human eye would naturally measure out a piece 120 centimetres in length.

2) Big Task String – used to mark out an area of earth for landscaping, create a clothes line or to tie someone up, this type would always measure 23 metres (give or take a centimetre).

3), 4) and 5) Ball of String – only ever available in 20- 50- or 100-metre rolls around the world, as the machines that produce string automatically cut it at these lengths to ensure there is never a piece of string of undefined length.

It is believed that the reason the lab assistant poisoned the Quartet and fled the country to open a strip club was that he was so disappointed by the results of his mentors' two-year study that he vowed not to waste any more of his life as a scientist.

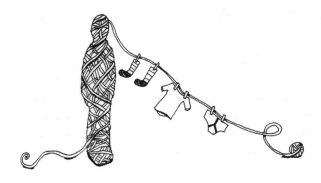

What would happen to a marshmallow man in a heatwave?

As summers have been getting progressively hotter, there have been rising concerns over what to do to safeguard the dwindling population of marshmallow men, for there is no doubt that a heatwave would have catastrophic consequences for these gentle creatures.

The Mallowmen of the salt marshes have a body make-up which is eighty per cent mallow, thanks to their marshmallow-rich diet. The root of this malvaceous plant, which can be identified by its pale pink flowers, yields mucilage which was originally the principal ingredient in marshmallow sweets, until a cheaper recipe using gelatin and sugar was devised. Mallowmen were almost made extinct when their food source was threatened by confectioners farming the marshmallow plant, but a small, protected colony still survives.

Mallowmen stay cool by keeping their fleshy pink bodies submerged in the shallow waters of the salt marshes for most of the day. In the event of a heatwave, however, these waters would recede, leaving them exposed to the elements. Those that weren't picked off by sweet-toothed fish eagles would soon begin to suffer the effects of the heat. First, their skin would begin to brown and crisp as it toasted in the sun. Then, as their body temperature rocketed, their mallow flesh would rapidly melt. One wrong move or a prick from a well-aimed barbecue skewer would be all it'd take to puncture their burning skin, allowing the gooey insides to spurt out and form a gloopy puddle on the marsh bed.

Conservationists in the area are on standby to apply lashings of sun cream and spray the creatures with a cooling formula should temperatures rise into the danger zone.

Is there anywhere I can get my hands on a magic carpet?

Trust us: you wouldn't want to. In almost every carpet shop in Birmingham there hangs a sign above the door which reads: 'We strongly advise customers NOT to attempt to perform any kind of experimental magic on our carpets.' Their warnings are justified, and their fears warranted. For centuries, magic carpets were the stuff of fairy tales and Arabian myths. That was until a Brummie carpet-seller on a business trip to Morocco unearthed an ancient Aramaic scroll while burying his host's pet hamster (which he'd accidentally sat on) in their garden. On returning home he got his business partner, who just happened to know Aramaic, to translate it. What he had discovered was an incantation; a spell written in verse which, when performed, promised to make small rugs fly.

Not believing what they read, the friends ignored the spell until one night they were passing their shop on the way home after a few too many beers and some dodgy kebabs, and figured it would be funny to try out the spell. They rolled out a large, seventies-style carpet (which they'd been planning on chucking anyway) and recited the words from the scroll, all the while trying not to laugh. All of a sudden, the carpet came to life and, as if drunk itself, began flailing about the room, destroying the window displays, knocking out one of the men and forcing the other to flee the building in fear of his life.

The door unlocked, the carpet was free to roam around the streets of Birmingham, leaving a trail of destruction in its path. But it being a Saturday night, and at the height of the binge-drinking summer season, most people mistook the huge carpet for a large bat, a low-flying aircraft or a figment of their alcohol-fuelled imagination. The rug never returned to Birmingham, and is occasionally sighted in other parts of the world, most notoriously in the Arctic where it was filmed lying flat on a glacier when a documentary crew showed up to catch a polar bear giving birth.

The incident shocked Birmingham's carpet industry to the core, as the two partners were widely respected in the business and many other carpet-sellers believed their story. What worried them most was that on that fateful night the incantation scroll was stolen from their premises by some opportunistic teenagers who saw that the door was unlocked. And so the signs were erected to dissuade any customers who may have come into contact with the scrolls from trying anything at home. Fortunately, so far the spell has not resurfaced, because if it did and carpets all across Birmingham started getting itchy feet and taking off, there's no doubt the Midlands would be in chaos.

How useful is a chocolate teapot?

As a tea or other hot drinks receptacle, a chocolate teapot would be pretty ineffective – if you used one you'd be likely to end up with one big sloppy, chocolatey mess on your mum's best tablecloth. However, it could come in handy getting you out of a tight spot, as the Belgian silk trader Martin le Choc discovered in China in 1845.

When Western countries first started trading with China, the people were very wary of Western ways corrupting their ancient and sophisticated culture. Traders travelling to the region had to do so under extreme caution, and often in disguise as Chinese farmers or tradesmen. There was no business more fraught and shrouded in secrecy than the silk industry, and so when Martin was sent to buy silkworm eggs from the troubled Qinghai region, he knew he'd need his wits about him.

After the successful negotiation and purchase of a batch of prime eggs, Martin embarked on his return voyage, only to be held up at gunpoint at the next village by a rival warlord who demanded that he surrender his cargo. Thinking on his feet, Martin offered to give him instead a treasure that would bring him far greater pleasure than all the wealth gained from 6,000 silkworm eggs. So saying he produced a packet of chocolate buttons which he happened to have in his pocket and offered one to the warlord to try. The warlord was astonished at the mouth-melting, exquisite flavour of the high-grade Belgian chocolate, and invited Martin back to his village.

But Martin knew he'd have to do better than that to impress the womenfolk of the village, and so when left alone to prepare for a ceremonial meal, he began to melt all of the chocolate he had with him and mould it into different shapes. At dinner the warlord's wives were astounded by the array of edible animals, trees and characters that Martin produced, but the first wife, who was a great lover of tea, was most taken with the exact replica of a Chinese teapot.

The warlord agreed to let Martin keep his shipment of eggs in return for this item, and provided that he continue to send them a regular supply of quirkily shaped chocolate goods. Relieved to escape, Martin set up a chocolatier's in Brussels after the sale of his silkworm eggs, and never returned to China again. And that is why you will hear Belgians praising something for being as useful as a chocolate teapot to this day, though, confusingly, the meaning is reversed when translated into other languages.

How do crystal balls see into the future?

Step aside, sceptics, and prepare to be amazed! A recent Department of Psychic Services survey has revealed that 65 per cent of crystal balls currently in action around Britain are of the future-predicting variety. That's up 5 per cent on last year's results. The increase is due to the number of fortune-tellers able to invest in a shiny new ball-shaped FIDD (or Future Information Dissemination Device), thanks to the help of increased bank lending and credit cards.

Crystal balls have been around since the 1700s when a small, bearded Romany man named Christoph Trente disappeared from his travelling family on a mission to find a way into the future. He isolated himself from the world and built a time machine out of twigs, berries and the carcasses of twelve woodland creatures on the top of the Italian mountain of Orteses (his exploits were related to his family in a series of cryptic postcards currently on display in Turkey's Museum of the Future). After seven years Christoph returned to his family with tales from the future to shock and surprise them.

But because of Christoph's lowly status, and the fact his family had fallen into disrepute in his absence, he was taken for a homeless fraud by the people of his home town. To try and convince the public of his adventures he set up a fortune-telling stall in the market square. He took with him a glass ball which he told passers-by could predict the future of anyone who dared to trust him. They would ask it a question, then, in the blink of an eye he would travel to the future and return with an answer to satisfy them. Slowly his reputation began to spread. To keep up with public demand he enlisted the help of family members, giving each a glass ball. Soon he was hearing tens, and later hundreds, of questions and travelling to the future to find the answers.

For centuries now, the time-travelling machine method has been passed down the family, as Romany Gypsies across the world happily paid through the nose to receive details of the future for their clients and themselves. Nowadays very few trips to the future are required because data is simply downloaded from the Internet of tomorrow onto USB devices, brought back, and distributed to the owners of Romany-approved crystal balls. This hasn't stopped fraudsters popping up all over the place (most notoriously in a small alcove on Dorset's Boscombe coastline, where customers were charged £100 for a thirty-minute reading) with fancy balls made from gemstones, often including phoney effects such as disco lights and dry ice. No true fortune-teller requires the use of their simple glass ball at all, just a high-speed Internet connection and a discreet earpiece feeding them all they need to know.

No man is an island, but is any man a mountain?

The largest man ever recorded was Piotr Stradovsky of the village of Bletchsenstien in the Czech Republic – but you won't find him in the *Guinness World Records* book. The invigilator who was due to measure him had her flight cancelled, and by the time she was transferred onto another plane out of London two days later the chronic liver failure which had plagued Piotr in his final weeks had taken its toll. Piotr's death meant he did not qualify for an entry in the book, but he was without a doubt the largest human being ever to have lived, and the Piotr Memorial Mound bears witness to that fact.

As a child Piotr had an insatiable appetite and his mother struggled to satisfy his needs. Living as he did on the traditional Czech diet of stodgy bread dumplings and pork knuckle with cabbage, he quickly piled on the pounds and was constantly bloated from his excessive wheat intake. He was showing all the signs of Prader-Willi Syndrome, but in the 1950s this condition was practically unheard of, and so nothing was done to curb his eating. By the time he was twelve he was the size of a Mini and still growing outwards, so his mother was forced to move him out into the barn.

He continued to consume vast amounts of food, and by his twenties he had burst out of the barn, his enormous belly towering above the roof of his mother's house. Well-wishers and those who wanted to see the Czech people receive world recognition for producing the largest human brought him a steady supply of food. But Piotr was slowly eating himself to death. Uncommonly for lifelong Prader-Willi sufferers, he survived into his fifties. He weighed a massive six tons when his organs finally gave up on him and he passed away.

The logistics of digging a grave for and burying such a massive corpse were a nightmare and so the regional council settled for covering him over with soil. Grass and flowers grew in abundance in the fertile ground and a little memorial garden was planted at the top of the mound. If you go to Bletchsenstien in the winter you can see small children tobogganing down its flanks – for the people of the Bletcheslav plains, Piotr's mound is the nearest thing to a mountain they have ever seen.

Do aliens eat breakfast?

Since the Men from Mars crash-landed in the Nevadan desert in the 1930s their eating habits have changed dramatically, but not how you may expect. Before that fateful day when an MfM scout ship muddled its coordinates and turned what was supposed to be a routine recon mission into a botched landing on Earthian soil, the little red men (surprisingly not green, because this way they camouflage better on their home turf) had a sophisticated diet that would impress any nutritionist.

Rather than agonising over a choice of breakfast cereals, what to snack on for lunch and where to go for a full hearty evening meal (like so many affluent Western Earthians) they were connected to a drip-feed system (similar to a hospital IV) which monitored their vitamin, sugar and water levels, feeding them appropriately and constantly throughout waking and sleeping hours. This way, they never felt hunger, never had to stop work to eat or pass waste products, and managed to cut carbon emissions dramatically over on Mars. These developments in their eating habits (it is believed there was a time, far ago in their history, when they feasted as we do) allowed them to speed up the evolutionary process and produce technologies capable of travelling further into our solar system than ever before.

But everything changed the day a crew of four found themselves wandering around Hokeyville, Nevada on the day of the annual Hokey Bake Fest; a full twelve-hour tradition where the town's people eat nothing but cakes and cream in a celebration of the famous Hokey Hot Bun (a muffin-like bread product, the recipe for which made the town a fortune in 1905 when it was bought by America's only cake supplier at the time and sold throughout the country in early convenience stores). Seeing the humans up close, feasting so happily at breakfast time on sugary delights, the MfM headed home intent on convincing their high council to change the planet's dietary regime, believing that a sugar-high breakfast must be the daily intake of a more advanced race.

After much debate, and surprisingly little experimentation for such smart creatures, the decision was made, and for a year they lived off daily marathon breakfasts consisting of nothing which wasn't topped with syrup, chocolate sauce or powdered sugar. Needless to say, no one has heard from them since.

How can I reverse evolution?

To reverse the process of natural selection in each and every living organism on planet Earth would be an impossible task for modern man, for he has not yet evolved the organisational skills required for such a mammoth project. To reverse the evolution of the *Homo sapiens* species itself, however, would be relatively easy, and in fact a group of eco-warriors in Finland are already testing the procedure on a small group of humans.

The hard-core Green Hero Squad are dead set on taking pollution down to zero, and will stop at nothing to achieve their aim. In an impassioned speech given chained to a tree outside the venue of the thirty-third G8 summit, Ossi Ollinaho, the leader of the squad, declared eco-war on the world's leaders, claiming that he had discovered a means to put an end to all industrial production. It's just a shame that no one heard exactly how he was going to do it as his parting words were drowned out by the sound of the chainsaws starting up.

By artificially deselecting the genes which have led to man's current stage of evolution, Ossi believed he could send the human race back into the time of the Neanderthals. In such a naive state we would no longer have the intelligence nor the dexterity required to invent, create or use the inventions whose emissions have steadily been adding to global warming. Whilst our feet would become bigger and hairier, our carbon footprints would grow smaller.

In the GH Squad experiments, the subjects are placed in a 'house' in which they are under constant surveillance by hidden cameras behind the walls and mirrors. They are provided with clothes to wear and food to cook each day, thus removing their need for independent decision-making, and given daily tasks which on the surface are 'team work' but are really a means of setting the subjects up in competition with one another. Under these circumstances the subjects become sexually territorial and the males begin competing to become the dominant male. Finally, as punishment for not succeeding in one of the tasks, the subjects are denied access to hair removal products and deodorant, allowing them to return to their natural state. At this stage, when their primitive urges are heightened, the brainwashing can begin and a psychic expert is brought in to hypnotise the subjects into believing that they are in fact Neanderthals – often money and tabloid magazine deals are used to influence them.

Once a breeding group had been set up in this way, it would just be a case of keeping them isolated until they had produced enough offspring to go forth and conquer the neighbouring settlement, and from there it would be only a matter of time before these stronger yet slower-witted beings became the dominant race.

Raindrops keep falling on my head – am I cursed?

Unless you live in the British Isles or the Amazon rainforest, where rain is pretty commonplace, there's a good chance you might be.

The servicemen and -women of naval forces throughout the world tell an extraordinary tale; the details vary from continent to continent but the basic premise, and inherent fear that exists within it, never changes. It tells of Petty Officer Julian Willson who joined the Royal Navy during World War One in order to escape a yawnsome job as a Morse code sound recorder based in Bognor Regis. The son of an Irish Druid, he was a quiet man who rarely spoke a word to the other officers and kept himself to himself. But the other officers didn't take to his shy nature and began to bully him, treating him terribly. He struggled on, taking the beatings and the name-calling, recounting all the details to his wizard father in a series of upsetting letters. Then, one day, most inexplicably, the skies turned grey above his crewmates' heads. Wherever they went, the darkness followed, constantly casting a shadow where they stood.

At first, the bullying officers found it amusing – after all, the shadows kept their beers cool on a hot day – but as time went on they began to pick on Willson, blaming him for the unusual clouds and bad weather and treating him worse than ever.

When the time came for their submarine, *HMS Courageous*, to leave for action, the captain decided Willson should stay behind as he would be bad for crew morale. So the boys left in high spirits, happy in the knowledge 'Weird Willson' was not going to be coming along for the ride and they wouldn't have to see the grey skies any more, as they'd be underwater. But alas, happy they would not remain, because on their fifth night at sea the heavens opened inside the control room, and spread throughout the vessel, raining down so hard they all thought the vessel was leaking. Signals were sent out to nearby crews relaying the message that the submarine had sprung millions of tiny leaks and that water was pouring through the ceiling like rain. The rain grew more persistent until the submarine flooded and sunk to the bottom of the sea, the entire crew perishing along with it.

The conclusion reached by the MoD was that the enemy had developed a new weapon capable of producing thousands of tiny holes in the submarine's armour... but Willson, who went on to be decorated for his wartime efforts and later wrote a book about his experiences, was less sure, believing his father to have cast a spell, cursing the other submariners for their cruel behaviour.

What does my front door think of me?

You've probably never taken much notice of your front door. For most it is a mere barrier between the inside and outside worlds, to be flung open and slammed shut at will. The most attention you are likely to pay it is if you are ever locked out and are forced to spend an hour staring at it blankly, possibly considering a paint job, as you wait for help to come. But rest assured that your front door notices you, and has thoughts and feelings all of its own.

Your front door only ever sees you when you leave or enter the house, so it must piece together an impression of your character from these moments. Let us paint a picture from the door's perspective:

On our first meeting you did not introduce yourself. Instead, you abused me by poking a key into my orifice and fiddling it around in there before finally pushing me open. You left me wedged in this uncomfortable position all day while you moved objects in and out, without so much as an explanation of what was going on. You never say goodbye when you go out, let alone tell me where you're going or when to expect you back. If you are in a bad mood you take it out on me by slamming me shut. When you come home drunk all I get is more prolonged poking, and covered in vomit if I'm particularly unlucky. You let strange men post things through my slit every morning and wait until I'm peeling before you think to protect me with a fresh layer of paint. And don't get me started on the strangers you let fondle my knocker!

The list of complaints could go on. A recent survey showed that eighty per cent of front doors would be content if their homeowners would just show them the basic common courtesies they would show any flatmate. Is it so much to ask? You might not really care what your front door thinks of you, but it is in your interests not to anger it. The old Irish superstition goes that if your front door slams shut of its own accord, it means there will be a death in the family. So, unless you're hoping to kill off any older relatives to cash in on your inheritance, you'd better change your ways and show your front door the respect it deserves.

How do I get out of sinking sand?

This depends greatly on the type of sand you find yourself stuck in. If it's 'slow' sand then your best bet is to move as little as possible and scream extremely loudly to attract attention, because the more you move, the further you'll sink. Aborigines have been known to last for a week in sand traps in the Australian outback by remaining perfectly still and just waiting for someone to stumble upon them and pull them to safety.

Sand of the 'quick' variety, however, requires a different self-preservation tactic. It is hard to spot due to its mud-like appearance – unlike the slower varieties, which tend to be sandy in colour and therefore stand out in non-desert environments – and is usually found in wooded areas. The sand is not actually sand at all, but a living fungus which works together with the earth surrounding it to generate a downwards pull so that it can absorb nutrients from the animals and plant debris that fall into its area, similarly to a Venus flytrap plant. The collecting spores of the fungus can grow to cover a forty-metre radius from the central point of the organism which lies buried deep below the topsoil. And it is outside of this spore area that you must get in order to ensure your survival.

Once you have stepped into the spore area you will begin to sink very quickly (a small Namibian child was reported to have disappeared into the ground in the space of two minutes while its mother ran for help), so as soon as you realise, take a deep breath and pull yourself down into the mud so you are totally submerged. The surface spores are the strongest, so if you can sink by a metre you will be able to pull yourself horizontally along as if in a swimming pool (breaststroke is known to be most effective). Provided you can hold your breath for long enough and you're not a terrible swimmer, you will gradually reach the outer ring of the fungus's spores where its pull is weaker and be able to drag yourself back up out of the mud to safety.

Another top sinking-sand tip, no matter what the type, is to fart profusely. As unsavoury as it may sound, the warm air pumped out repeatedly and at high pressure will heat up the earth around your body and loosen its grip on you, allowing you to claw your way to freedom.

How different are chalk and cheese?

According to a number of sources, chalk and cheese might as well be the identical twins of the food and natural composites family. One Oxford professor believes they're so similar he produced an entire language thesis on the way these two words came to mean 'extremely different' in our culture. What he discovered was that the phrase originated when a Devonshire schoolteacher, with a love for potent cheeses, named his identical twin sons Chalk and Cheese. Despite some dramatic personality differences – Chalk went on to be an Olympic rower and Cheese took to the stage as a comedian – the boys could not be told apart looks-wise by anyone that knew them. One day, during a school trip to the Houses of Parliament, a government aide heard the boys' father cheekily mention to a fellow teacher that the two main party leaders at the time were as different, on face value, as Chalk and Cheese; meaning that, superficially, they were very similar to each other. But the aide misconstrued what he heard and believed the phrase to be a perfect way to sum up the differences between the leaders, and drafted a statement for the press which expressed this. Soon, the phrase was in common usage up and down the country, with little thought for the fact that in various forms, chalk and cheese are pretty much the same thing.

In Cornwall there is a cheese shop which sells Olde Chalky, a popular crumbly cheese made of chalk deposits, fungi and cranberries. On a trip to southern Italy, you'd be in an unusual eatery if you didn't spot a calmercesco pizza on the menu – a locals' favourite topped with sun-dried tomatoes, chalk and basil. And up until 2007, when the government banned its use in schools on the grounds it could affect lactose-intolerant pupils, hardened cheese rind was used to write on blackboards as a more brittle, longer-lasting alternative to chalk. Unfortunately for powdered cheese manufacturers, if protestors have their way, the 2012 London Olympics could be the first competition to use real chalk instead of the powdered cheese substance as a slip-resistant agent for gymnasts to rub on their hands before competing.

Does time wait for any man?

Old Father Time has a fair old job on his hands, what with keeping all the clocks ticking and the egg timers timing simultaneously, monitoring all the different time zones and daylight saving systems, and celebrating the coming of the New Year 24 times on New Year's Eve (that's got to be a killer hangover). But since he was appointed in 153 BC he's done pretty well at his job, and in all that time has grown a beard to end all beards, stretching to just over a mile and requiring 500 fairies to keep it from trailing in the mud. He's the busiest man on earth, and has neither the time nor inclination to wait for any man.

Well, all right, maybe just one man… Every year, on Christmas Eve, Charles Pevensey Littlehands (for that is his real name – Father Time is just his job title) pauses time and puts up his feet for a well-earned rest. While his young, slightly fatter cousin Nicholas Claus frantically delivers toys to children around the world, Charles Egremont settles in by an open fire and reads the paper while Mrs Claus keeps him in good spirits with a steady supply of cookies and brandy and the elves take it in turns to rub his worn-out old feet.

Such are the strength of family bonds – you can guarantee that if any of us mere mortals requested a similar concession in order to squeeze a month's worth of revision into one night the answer would be a big fat no.

If you wanted to hold up time, you would have to find a way of temporarily obstructing Father Time from his duties. At the North Pole, where all the time zones converge, you can 'warp' time in a series of easy moves. If you take a jump to the left, then step to the right, then with your hands on your hips bring your knees in tight and do a pelvic thrust, you will find yourself face to face with the man himself. All you then need to do is grab a hold of his beard and reverse the steps to take you back to your original point in time, and time will have to stand still until you relinquish your hold on the beard. Of course, there's a limit to how much you can achieve whilst holding on to a Druid-convention's worth of beard, and the manoeuvre does come with a health warning: it can drive you insa-a-a-ane. But that won't stop you wanting to try it again.

Does Anything Eat Shit?

Eat Shit?

AND 101 OTHER CRAP QUESTIONS AND ANSWERS

A parody from the twisted mind of Sarah Herman

DOES ANYTHING EAT SHIT?

And 101 other crap questions and answers

Sarah Herman

ISBN: 978 1 84024 606 3   Paperback   £7.99

What would be more likely to survive a nuclear explosion - cockroaches or pickled onions?

They recently discovered the 'fat gene' - are there any others we should know about?

How many helium balloons would it take to lift me off the ground?

The world is full of really important questions. You will find none of them in this book. What you will find is plenty of nonsense, lots of lies and just enough truth to make you double check the 'facts' with a reliable source.

Following the huge success of the *New Scientist* books *Does Anything Eat Wasps?* and *Why Don't Penguins' Feet Freeze?*, this parody from the twisted mind of Sarah Herman is an alternative take on human curiosity. With detailed answers to ridiculous questions, if you've learnt absolutely nothing useful by the time you've finished this book, at least you'll be laughing.

'My favourite paperback title of the year'
                                        Paul Henderson, THE BOOKSELLER

'... will appeal to anybody who likes or has a slightly twisted sense of humour'   EXEPOSE magazine

www.summersdale.com